THE
ULTIMATE
BOOK OF
OUTFIT FORMULAS

A Stylish Solution to
What Should I Wear?

ALISON LUMBATIS

TEN PEAKS PRESS™

Cover and interior design by Studio Gearbox
Illustrations by Lydia Drye
Cover Photo © xcnova/Shutterstock

Ten Peaks Press is a trademark of the Hawkins Children's LLC. Harvest House Publishers, Inc., is the exclusive licensee of the trademark Ten Peaks Press.

The Ultimate Book of Outfit Formulas
Text © 2021 by Alison Lumbatis
Artwork © 2021 by Lydia Drye
Published by Ten Peaks Press, an imprint of Harvest House Publishers
Eugene, Oregon 97408

ISBN 978-0-7369-8208-5 (hardcover)
ISBN 978-0-7369-8209-2 (eBook)
Library of Congress Control Number: 2020055132

Printed in China

21 22 23 24 25 26 27 28 29 / RDS / 10 9 8 7 6 5 4 3 2

To my mother,
who taught me the power of
feeling good about my appearance.

And to my daughters,
who inspire me to do the same for them.

ACKNOWLEDGMENTS

Every word in this book was inspired by the Get Your Pretty On community. Thank you for your questions over the years. Although many times I didn't have the answers, I appreciate the grace you've always given and the opportunity to learn. Thank you for allowing me to share my imperfect journey with you. Special thanks also to...

Lauren Smith for being so much more than a business manager. You are my biggest cheerleader, my sounding board, and the best integrator on planet Earth. Thank you for always listening to my ideas and making them so much better than I could ever imagine.

Jessica Pigza for doing the research and being so much wordier than I could ever be. (Is wordier even a word? You would know!)

Lydia Drye for lending your talents to GYPO over the years and allowing me to bring them along on this journey. Your illustrations make this book shine!

Hilary Billings for unlocking the key to writing this book—trusting my gut. Thank you for encouraging me to infuse the DNA of GYPO into every page.

Kathryn Buchanan for your loyalty and for being with me since day one. I can *always* count on you to figure everything out.

Tiffany Howard for being on the front lines every day and giving our community virtual hugs through email.

Coty Adams for the multiple ways your creativity has elevated GYPO and its impact.

Ruth Samsel, Heather Green, and the entire team at Harvest House for believing in this project and lending all the support and love to make it so much more than just a book on fashion.

Crystal Gornto for holding space for me and showing me what it means to do it for others. Your friendship is such a gift.

Mindy Carter, JaNice Kloza, Cherrie Little, and Joseph Stingley for being my prayer warriors and constantly lifting me up on the days I needed it most.

My husband, Craig, and our children, Devon, Aubrey, and Ava—you are my greatest blessings. Thank you for always believing in and supporting all of my hairbrained ideas, dreams, and schemes. I told you one day they would pay off, right?

My Lord and Savior Jesus Christ for breaking me, redeeming me, and using me. You have ordained every step of my journey. I'm eternally grateful, humbled, and honored to be used in Your kingdom for Your purposes.

CONTENTS

Introduction..7

1 Back to Basics—Fashion 101..27

2 Making It Your Own—Define Your Personal Style......................41

3 Dressing Your Body Shape...49

4 Embrace the Outfit Formula...69

5 Dressing for Spring..89

6 Dressing for Summer...109

7 Dressing for Fall..133

8 Dressing for Winter..155

9 Dress It Up..179

10 Accessories and Footwear...199

11 Master-Class-Level Style...209

Conclusion...217

Notes..219

INTRODUCTION

I have to share a secret with you: I don't feel equipped to share style advice. I'm not a stylist by trade and have no formal training. This is an area of insecurity for me, which I think we can all agree is ironic since here I am, writing a book about style.

It's true—you're reading a style book from someone who is no more qualified to offer up fashion guidance than your trash collector. (Well, maybe a little, but there could be some stylish trash collectors out there, right? I'm open to the possibility.)

This feeling of unworthiness is a big part of how this book came to be. When I first started blogging, I honestly thought no one would ever want to read what I had to say. Why would anyone want to follow a work-from-home mom / telecom engineer who was putting together the most mundane, ordinary, casual outfits? Nothing haute couture or high fashion, but just some tees, jeans, and a couple of cute accessories? Turns out that's exactly what a lot of women were looking for, and there was definitely a need in the blogging world that I was able to satisfy.

First, let's jump in the way-back machine and set it to 1988, when I was 15 years old. That year, God whispered in the ear of a shy, insecure, bespectacled teenager with puffy sleeves (and even puffier hair) that one day He would use her to impact the lives of other women. Little did I know that He would take His sweet time doing it, and never did I ever imagine the way it would happen.

Twenty-five years later, it all came to fruition with a platform where I have the honor to serve hundreds of thousands of women and help them find confidence through easy style.

But we all know God rarely uses people in big ways without a few trials, and trust me, my friend, I wasn't exempt from the journey into the depths of a valley that led to this place. God has a knack for doing that, doesn't He? It's like He can't just say, "Here's your anointing; now go make it happen." No, He had to take me to that dark place—maybe because sometimes I don't listen all that well.

"Trust in the L<small>ORD</small> with all your heart, and do not lean on your own understanding. In all your ways acknowledge him, and he will make straight your paths."

—PROVERBS 3:5-6

MY YOGA-PANTS-MOM RUT

I now refer to that valley as my yoga-pants-mom rut, which is a cutesy way of categorizing a season of my life marked by depression and an utter lack of self-care. It was one of the darkest places of my adulthood.

My climb out of the rut is what led to starting my blog, *Get Your Pretty On (GYPO)*. Trust me, sweet sister, when I say that I've been there.

There and back.

Fun fact: I spent 14 years as a telecom engineer prior to accidentally stumbling down the path of style blogger. After I had prayed for many years to be able to work from home, my management changed, and I finally got the opportunity. At first, it was all sunshine and rainbows. Well, as much as being able to throw in loads of laundry in between conference calls can be. I trust you know what I mean. I was home in the morning, packing lunches and seeing the kids off to school, kicking butt at both my job and my household chores during the day, and driving a carpool for the afternoon pickup. Being able to work remotely and be at home with my kids had me fired up. I was living my work-from-home-mom dream.

This went on for a few months before I started to notice small, seemingly harmless changes. (You know, like how we all thought bangs would be a good choice. *Wrong!*) My closet, full of corporate clothes, was now obsolete. Instead of my favorite office outfit formula of a pencil skirt, blouse, and pair of heels, I slipped into my comfy black yoga pants and faded sweatshirt, pulled my hair back in a ponytail, and called it good for the day. Which would have been fine if I had been planning to do yoga (or anything else active). Instead, this became my new work-at-home-mom uniform. It's what I was wearing each morning when my husband kissed me goodbye and again when we greeted each other at the end of the day.

Hey, at least I wasn't spending all day in my pj's, so points for that! Honestly, I'm not sure that would have made much of a difference because I slid down the slippery slope into my rut anyway. Here's what that looked like:

First, I stopped working out.

Then fixing my hair flew out the window.

Followed by no makeup. (My husband loves me anyway, right?)

Close behind was not making healthy eating decisions, because of course I wasn't meal planning or cooking healthy meals.

Or doing laundry on a regular basis (hey, we were saving water), which led to piles of dirty laundry and a messy, disorganized home.

Which made me cranky with my husband and kids and led to no desire or energy for date nights or (dare I say it?) sex.

Until eventually I did not recognize the woman looking back in the mirror. My self-esteem was melting like a snowman on a hot day, and I was standing directly in the sun.

I woke up one day in the middle of a messy house, more than a few pounds heavier, and feeling disconnected from my husband, inadequate as a mom, and completely hopeless. I found myself wondering how things got to this point.

KEEPING HOURS

There's nothing quite like hitting rock bottom to light a fire of determination to make changes and make them fast. I decided to take a look at the things in my life I could control. The next morning, instead of my usual routine of sleeping until the last possible minute before the kids had to get up for school, I got up an hour before everyone else. Now, before you think self-discipline magically started to kick in, I was up early because I couldn't sleep with all of this weighing on me. With some extra time on my hands, I started my day with some prayer and devotion time and then set out to make myself an hourly schedule for the day. I've always worked well with a schedule, and I figured if I didn't have a job outside the house to help me keep hours, I could create this for myself.

I wrote out every hour of the day on a sheet of paper. My new morning routine looked something like this:

6:00 a.m.—devotions and prayer journal

7:00 a.m.—get the kids up, make breakfast, pack lunches, and drive
them to school

8:00 a.m.—work out

9:00 a.m.—shower and dress in *real clothes*!

I religiously stuck to my schedule and did all of the above with one small snafu. When I went to get dressed, I realized I had no real clothes to wear for my new work-from-home life—only a closet full of dust-covered relics from my corporate past life.

My first inclination was to go online to find outfit inspiration for work-from-home moms. Unfortunately, there wasn't much out there at the time. This was 2012 after all—a few years before the proliferation of every type of fashion blog imaginable. (Looking for ways to wear aluminum-foil outfits? There's a blog for that!) What I *did* find were some bloggers posting crazy-expensive designer outfits and wearing high heels that weren't going to work for my daily trips to schlep around Target.

So I decided to do something crazy and start my own blog. Did I know anything about blogging? Nope. Did I have any expertise to share? Nada. Zip. But I decided I could document my journey out of the yoga-pants rut and share what I was learning along the way. At that point, it didn't matter if anyone ever read it. It was something I needed to do for me. My husband and children obviously still loved and supported me in all things, but I was tired of feeling so out of sorts. I got myself into this mess, and I was the one who had to put the wheels in motion to get out of it.

It turned out that starting my blog was just the kick in the yoga pants I needed to establish some accountability and to get out of my rut.

MOMMY, YOU LOOK PRETTY!

So how did my blog get the name *Get Your Pretty On*? On the afternoon of that first day of my new routine, I picked up my daughter from school. She hopped into the car, gave me a once-over, and asked "Mommy, what happened to you?"

Not quite knowing what to say or what her angle was, I cautiously asked, "What do you mean?"

She said, "Well, you look *pretty* today!"

Did your heart just melt a little? Because mine did that day. It was kind of like a Grinch moment when my heart grew two sizes, and things have never been the same. (Cue Whoville music here: "Fahoo fores, dahoo dores...")

That, my friend, was my wake-up call, my day of reckoning, and the moment when everything changed. My self-neglect wasn't affecting only me. My daughter looked to me as a role model of what it means to be a wife and mother, and I hadn't been setting the best example. From that day on, I've tried most days to get dressed and stick to an hourly schedule. To say it's been life changing would be a gross understatement.

Let me say something important here. I'm not telling you that wearing yoga pants and a sweatshirt every day will lead you to this same place. There were a lot of factors that got me there. But taking small, tangible steps to get out of my rut was key. Getting dressed felt like one of the least overwhelming steps I could control. It changed the way I felt then and still does today.

Get Your Pretty On grew organically because at the time, there weren't a lot of resources out there for women like me. As a mom who struggled spending money on herself when there were gymnastics and horse riding lessons to pay for (Side note: Don't let your kids ride horses unless you really love being broke the rest of your life), I couldn't get on board with buying designer clothes that weren't practical for my daily life. Fashionistas recommended outfits outside my price point, comfort level, and relatability. (Who would spend $300 on a blouse when you had to make pasta for dinner and work on a paper-mache volcano after?)

> My self-neglect wasn't affecting only me. My daughter looked to me as a role model of what it means to be a wife and mother, and I hadn't been setting the best example.

As I shared my casual-outfit inspiration and what I was learning along the way, an audience of women flocked to the blog. They needed someone who was just *one step ahead* of them on the style journey. They weren't looking for a style guru or fashionista; they wanted another mom to show them how she was pulling off the at-home lifestyle and feeling beautiful on a budget. And friend, let me make one thing really clear—I am *not* a fashionista. I'm simply a mom who may be a few steps ahead of you on this journey. I've learned some things that make it easy for me to get dressed and feel confident in my clothes, and I'm sharing those things because I want you to feel the same way.

Need another reason to ditch your yoga pants? Studies have shown that what you wear positively influences your thinking, negotiating skills, hormone levels, and heart rate![1]

Over time, the blog has shifted in dramatic ways. Yes, I still provide budget-friendly, easy-outfit inspiration, but it's about so much more than that now. My main mission is to give you permission to feel pretty. If you're waiting for your husband or kids to tell you to go out and spend money on yourself, you may be waiting a very long time. (Trust me, I speak from experience! Your kids will only find ways to spend your extra money. See the horse-riding note above). You have that permission right now, and I'm here to give it to you. And that's anything *but* a vain pursuit. You deserve to live a beautiful life in every possible way.

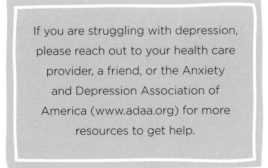

If you are struggling with depression, please reach out to your health care provider, a friend, or the Anxiety and Depression Association of America (www.adaa.org) for more resources to get help.

TALL POPPIES

If this is making you feel uncomfortable or bringing up some insecurities or other junk, then keep reading. Maybe you've been nodding yes this whole time but still know making a change is hard. So I think this is a good time to share a note I got from my friend Bebe, a midthirties stay-at-home mom who participated in our Outfit Formulas online styling program a few years back.

Alison, I can't tell you how much more confident I feel in my clothes now. It's so fun to put on a cute outfit every day, even if I'm not leaving the house. I'm so much more motivated, and it's spilling over into other areas of my life. My husband has even noticed! But here's a problem I didn't expect. Every week when I attend my moms' group, a few of the other moms say, "Why are you so dressed up?" The sad thing is, they're not saying it in a nice way, but in more of a "Why aren't you still in your sweat pants like us?" way. After a few weeks of this, I finally told them my secret—you and GYPO. I also invited them along for the fun. A few of them have started to follow along, and it's been a total game changer. We all feel good together. It's been such a treat watching their confidence soar. There's enough good for everyone, and sometimes it's braver to stand out in a good way than to blend in and stay stuck. It was scary to challenge the status quo of the "mom uniform," but now that I see what a difference it's made for all of us, I'll never keep you or GYPO a secret again!

I have a few friends in Australia who told me they refer to this as Tall Poppy syndrome. It's where we try to blend in with other women to make them feel more comfortable about themselves. We don't want to be the tall poppy sticking out above the others and making them feel inferior or "less than."

The thing is, those reactions and negative comments from others are about them, not about you. You're not responsible for anyone else's feelings, but why not bring your friends along for the ride? God created this world and all its beauty for all of us. He wants us to be the best version of ourselves. Instead of being shrinking poppies, this is an opportunity to pull our sisters up so we can all put our faces to the sun!

Action item: What is your "why"? Do you want to set a better example for your kids? Are you doing this as a way to get through the day? Remembering your "why" is a good insurance policy against any naysayers who may try to rob you of this experience. Instead of shrinking back, think of at least one woman you can invite along on the journey with you.

THE PROBLEM WITH MOTIVATION

You may be saying to me right now, "But I don't feel like getting dressed every day." That's perfectly fine. Let me share a life-changing secret with you:

You don't have to feel like doing something in order to do it.

(Record scratch—what the...*what*?)

Let me repeat that. You don't have to *feel* it to *do* it! Whoa, mind blown. See, that's the problem I have with motivation. If you're waiting to feel like doing something before taking action, it may never happen. This advice applies not only to getting dressed but also to many things you know you should be doing but just aren't feeling it—like eating right or moving your body or doing the laundry or (insert dreaded task here). *It's about creating a daily discipline and making a commitment to yourself whether you're feeling it or not.*

Here's another secret—sometimes when you take action first, *you feel it after.* Getting dressed is definitely one of those things. Putting on a cute outfit absolutely can change your outlook and the way you feel. I can't tell you how many times I wasn't "feeling it" but got dressed, put on a little makeup, and fixed my hair anyway. Just like magic, it works.

Every. Single. Time.

Dress the part, and you will feel it. You don't have to wait for the muse of inspiration to land on your shoulder. This is really good news, and research backs it up. Something called "enclothed cognition" proves that what we wear has a strong influence over the way we act and think. Two psychologists discovered this in a 2012 study when they had participants wear a white lab coat described as either a doctor's coat or a painter's coat. Those who were told they were wearing a doctor's coat had a heightened level of attention to detail and took on the same qualities they perceived doctors as having.[2]

What does this mean for us? Simply changing the way we dress can have a drastic influence on how we think about ourselves and can affect our levels of self-esteem and self-efficacy. Next time you pick out an outfit, think about how the clothes you wear could literally turn you into a different person. (Hmm...next time I may go for Catwoman.)

Let's say it together one more time because it's that important: *You don't have to feel it to do it!*

It's your turn: *Are you dressed yet? If not, let's change that right now! Pick out an outfit to spend your day in. It doesn't have to be fancy, just something that makes you feel put together and ready to face the day. Take notice throughout the day—how did your outfit make you feel?*

Were you more productive? More confident? Journal about
your experience to solidify your feelings.

FUN MATH?

As a mom, I can say with certainty that decision fatigue is real, y'all.
We are bombarded with tens of thousands of decisions a day. In case
you're wondering, according to several sources, that number is around
35,000.[3]

Thirty-five thousand decisions. *Every. Single. Day.*

I don't know about you, but just processing that wears me out a
little!

Alison's decisions this morning: Should I buy frozen chicken or fresh
for dinner tonight? Oops, no time to thaw—fresh it is! Actually, do I
even want to cook chicken tonight? Does the olive shirt or teal shirt
work better with these yoga pants? Does it even matter? Should Ava
go to the barn Tuesday and Thursday, or would Wednesday and Fri-
day work better? When should I schedule that call with her chemistry
teacher? How many hours should our new intern plan to work each
week? Do I want to attempt coloring my grays at home or wait a few
weeks to get into my stylist? Should we try to buy a house with a pool

this summer? Hmm...could I deal with the emotional toll of selling the house the kids grew up in? Should I get the mail now or wait until after lunch? Oh, wait...what's for lunch anyway—spinach salad or Lean Cuisine?

It's no wonder we're all looking for ways to make life just a tad bit easier. The popularity of "done for us" solutions, like delivery meal plans and personal style services in a box, speak to our desire to have someone else make the decisions or at least simplify them significantly. (I'm waiting for the Rock to create subscriptions to read our kids bedtime stories. It's coming. You heard it here first.)

That's a big part of why I'm on a mission to make getting dressed the easiest thing you'll do all day. How? By telling you exactly what to shop for and how to pair it up. My goal is to demystify the process of getting dressed by breaking it down into an easy formula anyone can use.

Few things make me happier than learning something that makes my life easier and then sharing it with all my friends. Remember? That's how this book came to be.

So, what is an outfit formula anyway? We'll get into this a lot deeper later on, but for now all you need to know is this—it's *fun math*! Yes, I said it. Fun math really does exist. Maybe you're already a math lover, but friend, I am not. The only time I love math is when it makes my life easier. Trust me when I say it's fun when used to create a foolproof formula for getting dressed that works for every body type, size, and age.

This book is chock-full of outfit formula inspiration for every woman— whether you're building your wardrobe from scratch or have a closet full of clothes and nothing to wear. These tried-and-true outfit formulas are some of my personal go-to's as well as favorites among *GYPO* readers and members of Outfit Formulas, my online styling program.

And just in case you're wondering what happened to that little blog called *Get Your Pretty On* that I started just for me, it turned out I wasn't the only one needing inspiration. It's grown into a platform where hundreds of thousands of women worldwide come to find confidence through easy style every day.

God has a way of doing things like that. I could never have planned a journey like this, and honestly, many times I've felt ill-equipped to be leading it, but every day He guides me to the next step. I couldn't be more honored to have you along for the journey.

After all, it's even better to feel pretty together.

BREAKING IT DOWN: THE OUTFIT FORMULA

After spending 14 years of my life and career as an engineer, I'm a little bit obsessed with creating systems for everything, and yes, that includes getting dressed. Thinking about putting outfits together in this way combines my right-brain logic with my left-brain creativity to identify foolproof outfits that truly work for everyone. Yes, I said everyone, and that means every body, every budget, no exceptions.

Let's back things up for a second. So, how did the first Outfit Formulas capsule wardrobe come to be, and what the heck is a capsule wardrobe anyway?

A few years back I sent out a survey to *GYPO* readers to ask if there was another way I could make getting dressed easier for them. I'd already been blogging for a couple of years and providing outfit inspiration on both the blog and social media, but I felt like I could be doing something more. When the survey results came back, lo and behold, there was a lot of overlap in the answers. My readers wanted a shopping list of pieces to go out and buy to build their wardrobes—including closet staples, classic items that would always be in style, and seasonal trends.

I was super excited when I saw this and more than a little eager to

Eliminating "Tolerations"

Since we are on the topic of sharing things that make life easier, I wanted to introduce you to a concept I learned several years ago that has changed my life for the better in small but significant ways. It's all about eliminating "tolerations" from our lives. What is a toleration, you ask? It's basically anything you're putting up with that drains your energy.

1. Identify Your Tolerations

Identify your tolerations and make a list. These are things that are frustrating, bothersome, or even annoying to you. For me last year it was a lumpy pillow. A pretty quick fix, but it's crazy how much not getting a good night's sleep affected me. I replaced it with a new pillow and immediately started sleeping better. That one change made my days that much better. Grab a piece of paper and start making your tolerations list, or you can use the Tolerations Worksheet from getyourprettyon .com/book to help you get started on your list.

2. Tolerations Are Not Long-Term Goals

Tolerations aren't long-term goals, but things that can easily and fairly quickly be taken care of. They could take five minutes or maybe a few hours, but they give you tangible results, and doesn't it feel great when you can check things off your list?

3. Take Your Time

Now, look at the list you made. You might be surprised to see that there are a few that you can immediately remedy and cross off the list. Put a star next to the two to four items that you want to start with. I promise you'll be amazed at how great you'll feel just getting those few things done. Next, you can set your goal. Do you want to tackle one toleration a day? Do you want to tackle a few a week? Whatever your goal, make sure it's attainable, and pick the items you want to accomplish that day or week. If you try to do it all at once, you may get frustrated or discouraged. Spreading it out helps with that. So what are you waiting for? Let's tackle those tolerations!

dive in to create this shopping list. I already knew the pieces in my closet that I wore most and that would make an awesome list of closet staples. Adding seasonal trends was a fun and easy way to inexpensively refresh those classic basics.

Once the list was complete, I thought, *What good is this list if I don't show people ways to pair up the pieces into outfits?* So I started to play around with each piece on the list until I had used each one in four or five different outfit combinations (or formulas). I accidentally created a capsule wardrobe without even knowing what I was doing! I'll never forget the first time a reader sent me an email saying, "I just love your capsule wardrobes, Alison!" I scurried to google the term "capsule wardrobe" as fast as I could because I didn't want to look dumb (at least not this time). In case I'm not the only one who's not familiar with this term, here's what I found on Wikipedia:

> **Capsule wardrobe** is a term coined by Susie Faux, the owner of a London boutique called "Wardrobe" in the 1970s. According to Faux, a capsule wardrobe is a collection of a few essential items of clothing that do not go out of fashion, such as skirts, trousers, and coats, which can then be augmented with seasonal pieces. [4]

Heck yes! I created a capsule wardrobe by accident! But in all fairness, I was part of the Garanimals generation. In case you're not as old as me, let me fill you in. Garanimals were clothing items for kids made to create mix-and-match outfits. All you had to do to create outfits was buy tops and bottoms with the same animal on the tag. Monkey shirts go with monkey shorts, lion shirts with lion pants...you get the idea. Easy peasy right?

Well, the Outfit Formulas capsule wardrobe program is basically this same concept, except it's for adults. We don't have pieces with animal tags, but I create the shopping list, and you check off anything you already have and shop for pieces to fill in the blanks. You can shop where you want and spend as much or as little as you want. Women shop everywhere, from thrift stores to high-end department stores. I also provide you with an online catalog of recommended items. Then, every day you get an email in your inbox showing you exactly which combination of the pieces to wear in your daily outfit formula. And voilà! Your outfit for the day is done like dinner.

All right, let's take a deeper dive into an outfit formula. Simply put, it's a combination of pieces that create a complete look. It's much like combining the ingredients in a recipe to create a meal. However, unlike meal planning, you can take liberties with these ingredients without totally ruining the dish.

If you think about the formula in mathematical terms, it's meant to be evaluated. (Don't worry—remember, this is *fun* math!) You can replace all the variables in it with specific values. For example, these variables:

jeans + T-shirt + cardigan + flats

can be replaced with specific values like these...

dark-wash skinny jeans
+ black-and-white striped
  T-shirt
+ red cardigan
+ leopard-print flats

white jeans
+ navy T-shirt
+ striped cardigan
+ strappy sandals

Each option still includes the variable of "jeans + T-shirt + cardigan + flats," but the details of each piece vary to create completely different looks. When you consider an outfit formula, look at your closet for specific values, and your outfit options become endless. You'll never say you have nothing to wear again!

Okay, so if math isn't your thing, then maybe food is. (Now we're speaking my love language!) Let's apply the analogy of "meal planning for your closet." Sounds crazy, but follow me here.

To get started, with each Outfit Formulas capsule wardrobe, you get a shopping list of "ingredients," or wardrobe items, for each season. Check your pantry, fridge, and spice cabinet. You'll have your staples in your pantry, perishables in your fridge, and in your spice cabinet, well, things that are going to spice things up!

In this analogy, your closet staples items will be items you can wear year-round, your perishables will be seasonal trends, and your spices will be accessories because they add some extra flavor. (See what I did there?)

Check off anything you already have on your list. Now we're going to the store (or shopping online) to fill in the blanks!

> An outfit formula takes the guesswork out of getting dressed by telling you exactly which type of pieces to pair up, and then you get to decide the specifics.

You're welcome to shop where you want and spend as much or as little as you want to get the remaining items. Armed with your list, head to your favorite store (or online retailer) to get the pieces you need. No more wandering around wondering what to buy or trying to figure out what is in style. Everything on your list will be paired up in a multitude of ways. That's what I call shopping with a purpose!

Once your shopping list is complete, it's time to combine the ingredients. Just follow the daily formula prompt to create the perfect outfit recipe. Don't forget to sprinkle generously with your favorite accessories to spice it up!

See? Easy peasy! If only parenting came with a formula.

HOW TO USE THIS BOOK

This book is meant to provide a springboard of outfit inspiration. The most fun part of personal style is just that—it's personal. Use these formulas to make an outfit your own and curate a personal style that you feel confident wearing. An outfit formula takes the guesswork out of getting dressed by telling you exactly which type of pieces to pair up, and then you get to decide the specifics. No matter what your personal style is (preppy, bohemian, elegant, chic, edgy...), you can use the formula to build an outfit from pieces that speak to you and create your desired look.

The formulas included here are timeless, classic outfits pulled from nearly a decade of tried-and-true *Get Your Pretty On* outfit formulas. They incorporate basic pieces that are not only flattering but also versatile and easy to wear. This makes it possible to shop your closet for these wardrobe staples and gives you the option to add in

Always remember that it's better to be a closet curator than a caught-up consumer. Don't feel pressured to buy something just to fill in a blank on your list; wait for an item you love. If it's not a "heck yes," it's a no!

seasonal trends as you like to elevate these timeless looks. This book also includes a shopping list for each season. You can check off the items that you already have in your closet and then purchase the remaining items as needed to fill in any blanks.

1

BACK TO BASICS—FASHION 101

Let's pretend for a minute that you're entirely new to the realm of fashion. I know most of us aren't, but just for fun, we're going to do a quick-and-dirty rundown of the main categories of apparel to set the stage for the remainder of this book.

There are so many options when it comes to tops, bottoms, dresses, outerwear, footwear, and accessories. This is not meant to be a comprehensive list but will give you a quick overview of the different pieces you may run across while building your wardrobe. This will also help to give you some context for pieces that will flatter your God-given gorgeous shape when we get to chapter 3, "Dressing Your Body Shape."

> "
>
> "I say, dress to please yourself. Listen to your inner muse and take a chance. Wear something that says 'Here I am' today."
>
> **—IRIS APFEL**

Tops

Let's start at the top with tops. From blouses to tunics and everything in between, there's no shortage of options to fit and flatter your upper body. Here's a visual dictionary with descriptions for some of the most popular styles of tops.

ASYMMETRICAL	BALLOON SLEEVE	BLOUSE	BUTTON-DOWN	CREWNECK
FLUTTER SLEEVE	GRAPHIC	HALTER	OFF-THE-SHOULDER	PEPLUM
PUFF SLEEVE	SLEEVELESS	SWEATER	SWEATSHIRT	TANK TOP
TIE-FRONT	TUNIC	TURTLENECK	V-NECK	WRAP

Dresses

Dresses are one of my favorite categories in my closet for one simple reason—they create an instant outfit! Who doesn't love a one-and-done item? Just throw it on with your favorite shoes, accessories, and a jacket or cardigan, and voilà—you're ready to face the day. Choose a style that highlights one of your favorite body parts. Here are some of the most common options.

A-LINE

ASYMMETRICAL

BODY CON

EMPIRE

HALTER

MAXI

PEPLUM

POUF

SHEATH

SHIFT

SHIRT

SLIP

STRAPLESS

SUNDRESS

SWEATER

SWING

TANK

TEE

TENT

WRAP

Bottoms

When it comes to your lower half, there's truly a silhouette to celebrate everyone's assets! Now that more options than ever are in vogue, you can confidently pick from any of these styles that best suit your body shape and personal style preferences.

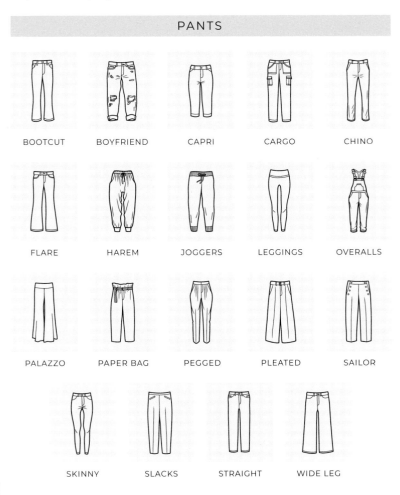

PANTS

BOOTCUT · BOYFRIEND · CAPRI · CARGO · CHINO

FLARE · HAREM · JOGGERS · LEGGINGS · OVERALLS

PALAZZO · PAPER BAG · PEGGED · PLEATED · SAILOR

SKINNY · SLACKS · STRAIGHT · WIDE LEG

A-LINE   CIRCLE   DENIM   MIDI   PAPER BAG

PENCIL   PLEATED   SLIT   STRAIGHT   WRAP

SHORTS

BERMUDA   CARGO   CHINO   CULOTTES   DENIM

DRAWSTRING   OVERALLS   SAILOR   PAPER BAG   TIE-WAIST

LAYERS

Jackets and cardigans add not only an extra layer of warmth to an outfit but also a lot of interest. If your outfit is feeling a little blah, try adding one of these toppers to kick it up a notch!

BLAZER

BOMBER
JACKET

CAPE

DENIM
JACKET

DUFFLE
COAT

FAUX FUR
JACKET

HOODIE

KIMONO

LONG
CARDIGAN

MILITARY

MOTO
JACKET

PARKA

PEA COAT

PUFFER COAT

RAINCOAT

SHORT
CARDIGAN

TRENCH
COAT

UTILITY
JACKET

WRAP COAT

VEST

FOOTWEAR

When it comes to footwear, there's just one rule to keep in mind—choose what works for *your* lifestyle. If you're a mom chasing toddlers, three-inch heels are unlikely to be your daily go-to, although they might be a fun option for date night. Likewise, if you work in an office most days of the week, you may need to have more dress shoes in your collection. Choose what works best for your daily life, and build your footwear wardrobe from there. Consider investing a little extra money for shoes, especially in classic styles that you'll be able to wear for many years.

ANKLE BOOT	BALLET FLAT	BLOCK HEEL	CLOG	D'ORSAY FLAT
ESPADRILLE	FLIP FLOP	KITTEN HEEL	LOAFER	MARY JANE
MOCCASIN	MULE	OXFORD	PEEP TOE	PLATFORM
PUMP	RUGGED BOOT	SANDAL	SLINGBACK	SLIP-ON
SNEAKER	STILETTO	T-STRAP	TALL BOOT	WEDGE

ACCESSORIES

Want to know the quickest and least expensive way to update everything in your wardrobe? Just add accessories! They're the icing on the cake, the gravy to your mashed potatoes, and the one thing that allows you to express your style personality and add visual interest to everything you wear. Even if you're a total accessory minimalist like me (hoop earrings and delicate necklace, all day, every day!), just adding a few small touches to an outfit makes a big difference in making it feel like a complete look.

BACKPACK

BELT

BRACELET

CLUTCH

CROSS BODY BAG

DROP EARRINGS

FLOPPY HAT

GLASSES

HEADBAND

HOOP EARRINGS

PENDANT NECKLACE

SCARF

SHORT NECKLACE

STATEMENT EARRINGS

STATEMENT NECKLACE

STUD EARRINGS

SUNGLASSES

TIGHTS

TOTE BAG

WRAP BRACELET

FASHION RULES—WHAT TO FOLLOW, WHAT TO BREAK

Rule #1: There's no such thing as age appropriate. Dress in what feels appropriate for *you*.

One of the questions I get asked most often as a style blogger is about dressing age appropriately, so I'm going to provide a little more context around this rule.

As a blogger over 40, I probably get this a little more than most. An internal alarm seems to go off when we hit 40 that makes us question what we're wearing. But whether you're in your twenties or your eighties, you may be wondering the same thing.

Here are some of the questions readers regularly ask: Can I wear ripped or distressed jeans? Are skirts above the knee off-limits for me? What about figure-hugging dresses, low-cut tops, or over-the-knee boots?

Being totally honest, I don't have the answers to these questions and am certainly no expert on this subject. But I *do* have a formula, a litmus test of sorts, that I use to arrive at my own conclusions.

But first, a little disclaimer. If I had to give my analysis on this topic, it would be that most of the Pretties (the members of the Get Your Pretty On Facebook group) err on the side of *not* dressing younger than their age. Which begs the question, are you dressing age appropriately if you're dressing *older* than your age? Is that any better? In your quest to look age appropriate, are you choosing things that make you look frumpier? Some food for thought!

Maybe the true question here

> Many of the style rules we were brought up with were from our mothers' and grandmothers' generations, and most of those guidelines need to be kicked to the curb.

is, should we even *be* "dressing our age"? My answer is a solid no. Instead, we should be asking ourselves these three questions:

1. *Does this make me feel more confident and stylish when I wear it?* Really, this is the most important question. If something makes you feel good, then wear it. If you're comfortable in it, and if you can look in the mirror and say, "This just feels like me," then you should absolutely wear it.

2. *Does this piece fit and flatter my body?* If a piece that feels "younger" fits and flatters you better than another item, then by all means wear it. We don't have to completely cover ourselves up to be age appropriate. As a matter of fact, in my opinion, it's always best to choose your favorite body part and show it off.

> We don't have to completely cover ourselves up to be age appropriate. As a matter of fact, in my opinion, it's always best to choose your favorite body part and show it off.

And this third question is what I call the gut check.

3. If you feel at all uncomfortable in it, then it's time to do a gut check. *What are my motivations for wearing this?* This is not for me to judge. We all know ourselves and what motivates our decisions, and if for any reason you feel icky when you examine it, then perhaps you ought to skip it and do a deeper dive into the feeling behind it.

At the end of the day, it comes down to two things. What makes you feel good? And what do you want to tell others about you with your clothes?

Rule #2: Dress the body you have now.

I can't emphasize this rule enough. One of the most frequent things I hear uttered from women new to the Outfit Formulas program is, "When I lose (insert a number) pounds, I'll be able to buy clothes." Embrace and dress the body you have now. Don't wait to see a number on a scale before you feel good in your clothes. Even if it's just a transition outfit that you buy with one pair of dark-wash jeans that fit you perfectly right now, you can wear those jeans every day and feel good in them. You deserve to feel good in your clothes now. That's what will help you want to get dressed every day. So go out and buy that one pair of jeans that make you feel good in the skin you're in. You have permission to feel good in your clothes *right now*.

Rule #3: Don't spend more than two or three days in a row in your yoga pants or sweats.

This is my own personal rule; it may differ for you. Years ago I discovered that if I spend more than two or three days without getting dressed in real clothes, the rut starts to deepen. It's my red-flag warning signal.

I'm very aware of this rule now and try to never, ever break it unless I'm sick or there's some other extenuating circumstance. Even on the days where I'm just really, really *not* feeling it, I force myself to shower, put on a little makeup, and get dressed. It's an instant mood booster, and it works 100 percent of the time. How can you argue with those odds? If you feel a rut forming, try it and see for yourself!

Having great style and feeling good in your clothes is not reserved for a specific size or weight. Stop waiting. Wear what you love now!

Rule #4: Your shoes don't need to match your belt or handbag.

Regardless of what Cher taught us in *Clueless*, it's actually more fashion-forward now to *not* match your shoes to your purse. Try out some fun combos with this—you could wear red shoes with a black purse, cognac shoes with a mustard purse, pink shoes with a taupe purse, brown shoes with a red purse...the possibilities are endless! It's far more fashionable to coordinate with complementary colors than to be matchy-matchy.

Rule #5: White after Labor Day is A-OK!

Many of the style rules we were brought up with were from our mothers' and grandmothers' generations, and this one definitely needs to be kicked to the curb. Wearing white after Labor Day is not only A-OK, it's also fresh, modern, and a great way to extend the wear of some of your favorite closet staples (white jeans, anyone?). I love pairing up my white jeans in the winter with soft pastel sweaters and neutrals.

Rule #6: You can wear navy and black together.

Don't be afraid to think outside the box when it comes to accessories! Consider a patterned watch strap, printed headband, or a small scarf with fringe as a fun way to add interest to your look.

Here's another rule carried over from the generations before us. This color combo looks especially smart when worn in an office setting. A navy sheath dress with a black belt and pumps is super chic and professional. You could also try this combo with a navy blouse and black ankle pants.

Rule #7: Mixing metals is more modern.

You no longer need to wear all gold or all silver jewelry. The more modern way is to mix your metals.

Layer necklaces in differing metals and styles to create a work of art around your neck. You can do the same with a bracelet stack that incorporates hues of both silver and gold. Add in a little rose gold for a fun twist!

Rule #8: Denim on denim works (if you follow one rule).

If denim on denim conjures up late '90s images of Britney Spears and Justin Timberlake, then you're not alone! Hear me out on this for a minute. Denim on denim (a.k.a. the Canadian Tuxedo) can be a great go-to combo, but you need to follow one simple rule—your denim washes must be in two different shades, one lighter and one darker. Think light chambray button-down shirt tucked into dark-wash jeans. This breaks up the all-over effect created by the acid-washed fashion faux pas of the past. Just like Britney and Justin, that was one breakup that needed to happen.

Rule #9: Fit matters more than anything.

I can't emphasize this enough. Wearing ill-fitting clothing that doesn't flatter our bodies is the biggest fashion mistake we're all guilty of. Whether it's pieces that are too tight or too loose, many women are walking around every day wearing items they don't feel good in simply because they don't fit properly.

A great-fitting piece of clothing should skim over your body in all the right places. It should never constrict, nor should it look too loose or baggy. Yes, it's hard to find clothes that fit perfectly, but please don't give up. Even an inexpensive piece

> A great-fitting piece of clothing should skim over your body in all the right places. It should never constrict, nor should it look too loose or baggy.

is worth spending a few extra bucks on to have it tailored so that it fits properly.

Rule #10: Pick your favorite body part to show off.

I'm speaking to two camps here. Camp 1 shows off all their assets in one outfit; camp 2 completely covers them. Let's aim for camp 1.5—something in between. Do you love your shapely shoulders? Wear a sleeveless top or dress to show them off. What about your long legs? You definitely want to wear more skirts and shorts. Highlight your one favorite body part in each outfit, and you can't go wrong.

2

MAKING IT YOUR OWN—DEFINE YOUR PERSONAL STYLE

Personal style is really hard to address because it's so, well, *personal*! It took me many years to figure mine out, and in some ways, I'm still a bit of a split personality. But I will tell you this: I could pick up on many clues, including some that went all the way back to when I was a teenager. I always leaned toward more classic styles and was never all that cutting-edge. Sure, I loved a good seasonal trend and added them in each year, but my style always leaned a bit toward the classics and still does.

YOUR FIRST CLUE

I had to step into my magic time machine to help determine my personal style, and you may need to do the same. It's time to become your own personal style detective! Our leanings in our youth can help us glean some clues and insights into what our personal style preferences are. But unlike personality, this is not necessarily a fixed trait that stays the same over time. There may have been some phases you'd rather forget, and that's perfectly fine! You can wake up tomorrow morning and decide that your fashion personality is totally different. There are no rules or right-or-wrong answers here. It's all about what makes you feel most confident and comfortable and what feels like a true representation of who you are. Fashion is such a fun way to share with the outside world important information about how we want to show up.

FINDING YOUR PERSONAL STYLE

There are hundreds of online quizzes to help you determine your style, but I'm all about simplifying processes for you, so let's cut right to the chase. This three-step process will give you important clues and provide powerful insights into your own personal style vibe.

> Personal style is all about what makes you feel most confident and comfortable and what feels like a true representation of who you are.

Some books and resources do a deep dive into determining your personal style personality, but I like to keep things a bit looser. I might start a week as a trendsetter, the next day be a total minimalist, and the day after that rock some boho vibes. I don't think we need to fall into strict categories when it comes to defining our style. Instead of assigning categories, I encourage you to go through this process to create a personal style framework that works for your unique situation and lifestyle.

1. Gather intel.

Become a style detective. Build your case by going online and searching outfits on Pinterest or Google. Create a file folder on your desktop or a new board on Pinterest of outfit ideas you love. At this stage, don't think deeply about why you like the look, just do it. Aim for 25 to 50 outfit ideas so you can get a much clearer picture of what appeals to you and patterns can start to emerge. As you scroll through them, look for commonalities. Are they minimalist, trendy, classic? Do they employ similar colors? Brights or neutrals? What about patterns? Do you tend to steer clear of lots of detail and interest, or are the outfits you chose full of them? Pay attention to shoes and accessories too.

2. Determine your lifestyle.

Personal style doesn't work for anyone without taking lifestyle into consideration first. For instance, you can love pencil skirts and high heels all day long, but if you work from home (raises hand), these are not practical items. Yes, I still love these pieces and even have them in my closet, but I know they're reserved for work conferences or special occasions. In my daily life, it's more important for me to look put together, yet comfortable enough to work from home and occasionally make a Target run.

That's not to say I can't stamp my personal style on these work-from-home outfits. I lean toward classics with a few fun trends added in, so you'll find me most days in a half-tucked slouchy tee paired with the latest denim trend, topped with a cardigan, denim, or moto jacket and finished out with comfy flat shoes (mules or slip-on sneakers) and minimal accessories (gold hoops and a short necklace). It's a uniform that works for me almost every day of the year, and it just feels like, well, *me*.

3. Curate confidently.

Around Get Your Pretty On, we have a saying: "We are closet curators, not caught-up consumers." This means we slowly and deliberately build our wardrobes from pieces we love that make us feel confident every time we put them on. Building your wardrobe should never be about buying an item simply to fill in a gap. If it's not a "heck yes," it's a no. When in doubt, do the selfie test. A selfie never lies! Either in the fitting room or at home, snap a quick mirror photo of your outfit. If the piece doesn't work for you, your selfie won't whisper lies into your ear and tell you that it does (unlike your husband or kids...although kids *can* be brutally honest sometimes). At the end of the day, your outfit needs to not only represent who you are but also make you feel confident and beautiful.

THE SELFIE NEVER LIES

As I said, if you really want to know how something looks from an objective point of view, take a selfie. A selfie is a quick and easy way to help you determine if an item or outfit is a "heck yes" or a no. If you still can't decide after viewing your picture, a quick message to a trusted friend is just a few clicks away. Below are some tips to help you take a selfie that will help you in your decision-making process.

"Style is a deeply personal expression of who you are, and every time you dress, you are asserting a part of yourself."

—NINA GARCIA

1. **Experiment with angles.** If at all possible, keep your camera at face height (or higher) and tilt it down to capture your outfit. It's a more flattering perspective and will slim your face.

2. **Look for great lighting.** Natural outdoor light is usually best. Make sure your light source is in front of you. If it's behind you, you'll be cast in shadow, and your photo will be dark and hard to see.

3. **Smile, but control it.** A nice small, natural smile is best. A smile is your best accessory!

4. **A camera timer or Bluetooth remote** is extremely helpful.

5. **Try the "shelfie"** by putting your phone in a clear cup on a shelf and use a timer.

6. **Don't stand straight toward the camera.** Position your body at an angle and bend a knee and arm. This always helps your posture.

7. **Try not to block your face.**

8. **Selfies don't require hair and makeup.**

9. **Crop out as much background as possible.**

10. **Take several selfies and pick out the best one.**

PERSONAL STYLE TYPES—WHICH ONE IS YOURS?

You may find that even though you don't fit neatly into a particular style category, some characteristics of it appeal to you. There are 101 different style types on the internet, but I like these four main categories as defined by Style Yourself Chic's Megan Larussa. [5]

Classic. In case you're wondering, this is my category. As Megan describes it, it's more of a catchall or umbrella for many different types of classic, including ladylike, preppy, menswear, and French and English classic. This category is all about fit and pieces that stand the test of time, although trends are incorporated to keep it all fresh. Style icons in this category include Audrey Hepburn, Jackie Kennedy, Grace Kelly, and Kate Middleton.

Bohemian. Popularized in the hippie movement of the '60s and '70s, Bohemian (or boho) is free-spirited and has a flowy, less tailored vibe. Think peasant skirts, embroidered tunics, flowy kimonos, crocheted vests, and fringes on everything. Bohemian style icons include Kate Moss, Cher, Zoë Kravitz, and Stevie Nicks.

Minimal. Although classic style holds the biggest piece of my heart, minimal also really speaks to me. Defined by clean lines, fuss-free accessories, and a mostly neutral color palette, minimal is more understated. Pieces should be perfectly tailored and well made. Gwyneth Paltrow, Sofia Coppola, and Coco Chanel all fall under the minimalist category.

Eclectic. If you're looking for next-level style, this is your category. Eclectic incorporates all of the personal style categories in one look. It's artistic and takes into account design, style, and details. Eclectic dressers may hold on to their favorite pieces for years, always finding new ways to pair them up. Style icons in this space include Sarah Jessica Parker, Katy Perry, and Helena Bonham Carter.

LIFE STAGES AND REINVENTING YOUR STYLE

Many of the women who come to *GYPO* find me because they are in some sort of transition phase of their lives. Some were stay-at-home moms but are now working outside of the home. Others are rebuilding their wardrobe after a pregnancy or weight change. Some are empty nesters looking to reinvent themselves in some way. Many of them are like me—exiting an office job and not quite sure what to wear for a new work-from-home or stay-at-home lifestyle. You need to consider what your new lifestyle or stage consists of and accept that your old wardrobe just may no longer fit the bill! Is this easy? No, not at all. But I promise it will be worth it.

Do you have a signature style item? If not, let's find you one! It could be some funky eyeglasses, statement-making shoes, or a bold accessory. Try out a few items and see what feels most like *you*.

I want you to know this: You deserve to have a wardrobe that works for your life right now, just as you deserve to have clothes that fit your body right now. Your clothes need to fit your lifestyle and work for this stage. You are no longer the person who wore those old clothes—in one way or another. Honor and release the purpose they served.

Don't use the excuse that no one is going to see you anymore or that you're not worth the time, effort, or money required to rebuild your wardrobe. Even a smallish wardrobe full of pieces you love and can mix and match to create outfits is sufficient to get you through the days. Just know that your life stage right now deserves to have a wardrobe that works for it!

***It's your turn:** Go online today and find at least 25 outfits that appeal to you. Call up a friend and ask her to do an analysis for you to detect patterns in the outfits that you selected. Bring the chilled rosé and do the same for her!*

DRESSING YOUR BODY SHAPE

One of the guiding principles of everything I do at Get Your Pretty On has always been to make style inclusive—that means every body, every budget, no exceptions. Our community is a beautiful representation of every God-given shape and size, and that's what makes it so unique and special. Enjoying fashion and feeling good in your clothes isn't just for women who weigh a certain amount or appear on social media. One of the tenets of the Outfit Formulas program is that you deserve to feel good in your clothes and to dress the body you have right now. You are excellently formed and marvelously made, exactly how the Master Artist created you, so celebrate your uniqueness! Once you have determined your body shape, you'll clearly see how each outfit formula can be applied for petites, plus sizes, and everyone in between.

> You deserve to feel good in your clothes and to dress the body you have right now.

That's why determining your body shape is important enough to get its own chapter. Even if you think you already know what yours is or you don't feel like doing the work in this chapter, please don't skip it. What you learn and determine here is going to guide your choices and shopping decisions as we work through this book. Yes, it's going to involve a teensy bit of math, but hey, they are called outfit formulas after all, so you already knew what you were getting yourself into. Remember, all math in this book is fun math!

Determining your body shape can open up many doors in the world of clothing. It's not about hiding what you've got, but about accentuating what you love. That's right—we're going to show them what you're working with (crank up your favorite rap song here)!

Body shape is determined by four basic measurements: shoulders, bust, waist, and hips. But these aren't the only factors to consider. Equally as important is where you carry your weight and tend to initially gain or lose weight.

Identifying your best physical features makes it easy to know exactly what to highlight when selecting pieces for your outfit. Play to your strengths, and you'll never go wrong!

All right, it's time to dive into that fun math I promised you! For this next part, I'm going to need you to grab a measuring tape, pencil, and paper and get naked (or nekkid, as we say here in the South). Sounds fun already, right? Seriously, in order to take accurate measurements, you must be either naked or wearing tight-fitting clothes, such as leggings and a cami. It's also recommended that you don't wear a bra when taking measurements so you can get them as accurate as possible.

Let's begin.

BODY MEASUREMENTS

Shoulders. You may need to have someone help you with this measurement. Pull the tape tight around the tops of your shoulders almost to the point where it slips off.

Bust. When measuring your bust, make sure the measuring tape is straight across your back and at the fullest point of your bust. Do not pull the tape too tight when taking your measurements, but make sure it is pulled snug.

Waist. When taking your waist measurement, be sure to measure around the narrowest part of your waist—not where your belly button is, but just a little higher. Again, pull the tape taut but not too tight.

Hips. When measuring your hips, make sure to measure at the widest part, which for most women is around the level of their crotch, below the hip bones and around the largest part of your butt.

BODY TYPE

Now that you have written down all these numbers, let's figure out your body shape. There are four main body shapes. You may have heard them referred to as fruits and veggies, like apples, pears, and carrots, or as shapes, such as triangles, rectangles, and squares. The names are interchangeable; just remember that triangles are pears, inverted triangles are apples, rectangles are athletic, and hourglasses are curvy.

Clear as mud? Don't worry, it will all make sense. Let's take a look at your numbers and find out which of the four basic body types you fit into.

 If your hips are wider than your shoulders, then you're a **triangle**, or **pear** shape.

 Are your shoulders or bust wider than your hips? You're an **inverted triangle**, or **apple** shape.

 If all four measurements are the same or very similar with no defined waistline, you're a **rectangle**, or **athletic** shape.

 If your shoulders and hips are about the same size with a defined waist, your shape is **hourglass**, or **curvy**.

If you're not 100 percent sure and want to get really mathematical, try this. A fashion expert named Bradley Bayou developed some equations to help double-check that you landed on the correct body type.[6]

You are a triangle (also known as pear) if your hips are more than 5 percent bigger than your shoulders or bust (hips divided by shoulders or bust ≥ 1.05).

For example, you are a triangle if your shoulders are 36 inches and your hips are 37.75 inches or larger.

You are an inverted triangle (or apple) if your shoulder or bust measurement is more than 5 percent bigger than your hip measurement (shoulders or bust divided by hips ≥ 1.05).

For example, you are an inverted triangle if your shoulders are 36 inches and your hips are 34.25 inches or smaller.

You are a rectangle (athletic build) if your waist is less than 25 percent smaller than your shoulder or bust (waist ÷ shoulders or bust ≥ .75) *and* your shoulder, bust, and hip measurements are within 5 percent of each other.

Find this out by looking at your shoulder, bust, and hip measurements. Call the largest of the three measurements t (usually it will be your shoulders) and the other two measurements y and z. Multiply t by 0.95. If y and z are greater than the result of t x 0.95, then your shoulders, bust, and hips are within 5 percent of each other.

For example, you are a rectangle if your shoulders are 36 inches and your waist is 27 inches or more.

You are an hourglass (or curvy) if your waist is at least 25 percent smaller than your shoulder or bust (waist ÷ shoulders or bust ≤ 0.75), your waist is at least 25 percent smaller than your hips (waist ÷ hips ≤ 0.75), *and* your shoulder and hip measurements are within 5 percent of each other.

Find this out by looking at your hips and shoulder measurements. Call the larger of the two measurements t and the smaller of the two measurements y. Multiply t by 0.95. If y is greater than the result of t x 0.95, then your hips and shoulders are within 5 percent of each other.

For example, you are an hourglass if your shoulders and hips measure 36 inches and your waist is 27 inches or smaller.

Didn't think you were ever going to use those multiplication and division skills after high school, huh? Don't worry, you can put your pencil down now.

Now that you know your body shape, let's talk about some general rules when it comes to choosing clothing items that will fit and flatter you.

Important note: This guide is to be used as a starting point.

It lists best bets for each body shape, but these are not meant to be hard-and-fast rules. You might be able to wear pieces suited for other body shapes and still look and feel amazing. For example, I'm a triangle (or pear) body shape, which means dark-wash boot-cut jeans would be most flattering, but I'm totally #skinnyjeansforlife!

Also, don't be discouraged if you don't neatly fit into any one category. We may fit into two different body shape categories, and that's OK! It's possible to have a primary body shape as well as a secondary one. The key is to play up the parts you want to highlight. Bodies come in all shapes and sizes, and your unique body shape might be flattered by pieces in more than one category. Play around with pieces, and remember to take selfies of each item. With a little trial and error, you'll be able to determine the pieces that fit and flatter your body the most. If you're really struggling to find your body shape, try simplifying the equation by using only your bust, waist, and hip measurements. Need a little more help? Join the Get Your Pretty On Pretties group on Facebook. You can find a link to it at getyourprettyon.com/book.

Outfits are all about balance, and learning your body shape can help you take that to the next level. Let's explore how we can create this balance in each of the following body shapes.

THE TRIANGLE STYLE GUIDE

Triangle shapes typically want to add more volume to the top, emphasize the waist, and de-emphasize the lower body in order to create that balance. This will also help to draw the eye up.

Superpower: You look awesome in every style of jeans!

Secret weapons: Patterned tops that accentuate your waist, shoulders, or back. Bold accessories that draw the eye up, like statement earrings and necklaces.

Tops: V-necks, cowl-necks, scoop necks, bell sleeves. Fitted tops to accentuate narrow shoulders and waist, any sleeve length or style.

Bottoms: Boot-cut pants and jeans or flares with heels to elongate legs, darker solid colors.

Jackets: A-line, princess cut, waist length, any jacket or coat that hits at mid-thigh, cropped styles.

Dresses: A-line, maxi, belted, open back, dropped neckline, hemlines below the knee to elongate legs.

Steer clear of: "Whiskering" on jeans across your hips, pleated pants, horizontal stripes on your lower half. All of these will draw the eye to the widest part of your body and throw off your proportions.

THE INVERTED TRIANGLE STYLE GUIDE

To achieve balance, an inverted triangle will typically do the opposite of a triangle and opt for adding volume on the bottom half rather than the top. This plus a defined waist help to create curves and showcase a balanced silhouette.

Superpower: That full bust and those amazing legs!

Secret weapons: Long, layered or pendant necklaces that elongate your frame.

Tops: Flowy tunics, breezy A-lines, relaxed button-ups, and V-neck everything. Any sleeve type or length.

Bottoms: Skinny jeans, leggings (especially when paired with tunics), flares with heels, boot cut, trouser fit, cropped or ankle pants, structured pants with flowy tops to balance the look.

Jackets: Vests, coats, or jackets that hit at the hip or upper thigh. A-line coats or straight knee-length style coats without belts.

Dresses: Strapless, maxi dresses with a lower neckline, wrap dresses, minidresses, and sheath styles.

Steer clear of: Heavy waist belts, empire-waist tops, anything form-fitting over the belly.

THE RECTANGLE STYLE GUIDE

Much like the hourglass shape, the rectangle is already very balanced on both the top and the bottom. However, the key to a rectangle shape is to break up this balance ever so slightly by creating a defined waist.

Superpower: Your well-balanced figure looks great in just about anything. Lucky girl!

Secret weapons: Pick the part of your body you like most and highlight it. It can be your muscular arms, defined shoulders, waist, or legs.

Tops: Halters, racerback, scoop and round necklines, strapless, any sleeve length or style.

Bottoms: Skinny jeans, leggings, trouser style, floor grazing for elongation, wide leg.

Jackets: Fitted, structured styles. Cropped styles, pea coats, long duster-style coats. A-lines and hems that hit at the hip or below the knee.

Dresses: Most styles work, so choose what you want to play up. To show off your legs, pick a shorter hemline. To play up your bust, choose strapless dresses. Skirts of any length work. Add a thin belt to create a waistline.

Steer clear of: All-over volume. If you pick breezy, wide pants or skirts, select a more form-fitting top and vice versa.

THE HOURGLASS STYLE GUIDE

The hourglass shape is naturally balanced, and the key to dressing it is to avoid losing that balance. Try to keep your top and bottom proportions even and your waist defined.

Superpower: That waist, those curves! Pick what you want to flaunt. The world is your oyster!

Secret weapons: Skinny belts worn at the waist. Necklaces that hit at your collarbone.

Tops: Form-fitting tops, wrap tops, and peplums. V-neck, scoop neck, round neck, or boatneck. Any sleeve length.

Bottoms: High waists, flares with heels, low-rise hip huggers, stretchy skinny jeans, and leggings.

Jackets: Classic belted trench, fitted blazers, cropped jackets.

Dresses: Wrap dresses, fit and flare, A-line. Deep V-neck. Anything belted that accentuates the waist.

Steer clear of: Boxy or flowy styles without definition. Belt a flowy top or dress.

TRIANGLE BODY SHAPE GUIDE

SHIRTS

BUST POCKETS	CROP	RUFFLE	STRIPES	WRAP BUST

SLEEVES

BATWING	BELL	CAP	FLUTTER	PUFF

NECKLINES

BATEAU	COWL	OFF-SHOULDER	SABRINA	SQUARE

PANTS

BOOTCUT FLARE HIGH-RISE STRAIGHT WIDE

DRESSES

A-LINE EMPIRE TULIP WRAP X-LINE

JACKETS

CROPPED BOMBER CROPPED DENIM LONG BLAZER LONG SHEARLING TRAPEZE

COATS

A-LINE EMPIRE LINE PRINCESS TRENCH WRAP

INVERTED TRIANGLE SHAPE GUIDE

SHIRTS

FITTED FITTED TEE PEPLUM TRAPEZE WRAP

SLEEVES

DOLMAN DROP SHOULDER KIMONO RAGLAN WIDE STRAPS

NECKLINES

ASYMMETRIC HALTER SCOOP U-NECK V-NECK

PANTS

BAGGY BOOTCUT BOYFRIEND FLARED WIDE

DRESSES

A-LINE NIPPED WAIST PANELLED WAIST PLEATED SHIFT

JACKETS

BELTED BLAZER CUTAWAY HIP DETAILS WATERFALL WRAP CARDIGAN

COATS

A-LINE CAPE COCOON PRINCESS TRAPEZE TRENCH

SHIRTS

| BELTED | BUTTON-DOWN | PUSSY BOW | RUFFLE | WRAP |

SLEEVES

| CUFFED | FLARED | FLUTTER | PUFFED | ROLLED-UP |

NECKLINES

| BATEAU | OFF-SHOULDER | SCOOP | SWEETHEART | V-NECK |

PANTS

BOOTCUT | SKINNY | SLIM | STRAIGHT | WIDE

DRESSES

EMPIRE | PRINCESS SEAMS | SHIFT | WRAP | X-LINE

JACKETS

BELTED | DOUBLE BREASTED | PEPLUM | STRAIGHT | STRUCTURED

COATS

DUSTER | PEACOAT | STRAIGHT CUT | TRENCH | WRAP

HOURGLASS BODY SHAPE GUIDE

SHIRTS

BELTED	FITTED TEE	FITTED SHIRT	FITTED WRAP	PEPLUM

SLEEVES

3/4	BISHOP	FITTED	SET-IN	SLEEVELESS

NECKLINES

OFF-SHOULDER	SCOOP	SQUARE	SWEETHEART	V-NECK

PANTS

| BOOTCUT | FLARE | SLIM | STRAIGHT | WIDE |

DRESSES

| BIAS | PANELLED WAIST | PEPLUM | SHIFT | WRAP |

JACKETS

| BELTED BLAZER | BELTED CARDIGAN | FITTED BLAZER | FITTED LEATHER | SHORT |

COATS

| A-LINE | COACHMAN | PRINCESS | TRENCH | WRAP |

65

TIP: As you review each season's shopping list throughout the remainder of this book, refer back to this section when applying the outfit formulas to your body shape. This will help to identify the pieces, cuts, and styles that will flatter your particular body shape. For instance, if you're an hourglass (or curvy) shape shopping for a striped top, you may want to choose a form-fitting V-neck as opposed to a flowy one that an inverted triangle (or apple) might choose. In this example, your dark-wash jeans could be high-waist flares.

It's your turn: Are there any pieces in your closet right now that you know don't fit and flatter your body? If so, pull them out to donate or sell.

CELEBRATE YOUR BODY

Talking about our bodies is tricky because we bring so much emotional baggage to the conversation. I railed against my triangle-shaped body type for far too many years, longing to be an athletic rectangle and trying my hardest to whittle down my curves, whatever it took. I dieted, worked out, and followed all the advice I could find before finally accepting and eventually loving the curvy body God blessed me with.

Please know this. Your value and your worth have nothing to do with the tag in your clothes or a number on a scale. They already reside within you, so you don't have to earn them or prove them to anyone.

Consider why you feel the way you do about your body. Is it because of years of cultural messaging or a comment your great-aunt Martha made 25 years ago? Do you feel dissatisfied with your body? Do you think you are *supposed* to feel that way because of messages that have been shoved in your face for years? As retailers sell clothes with inconsistent sizing and the media posts heavily photoshopped ads, the mainstream definition of beauty is a moving target that is impossible to hit. And honestly? It's exhausting.

You have permission to accept your body just as it is at this very moment. It's OK to love and be proud of your body as it is right now. No one's body is perfect or was ever meant to be. Your body is meant to serve you. Show it the respect and appreciation it deserves for empowering you to hold your children, walk along the beach, and carry out your daily activities.

> "You have been criticizing yourself for years and it hasn't worked. Try approving of yourself and see what happens."
>
> **—LOUISE HAY**

It's your turn: Start following social media accounts of women who look like you. Take the time to regularly connect with your body through mindful movement, such as yoga, Pilates, or tai chi. Write down the ways your body has served you, and repeat them as positive affirmations regularly. It takes time and mental work to transform the internal narrative you've believed for many years, but it can be done.

ALISON'S AWESOME ADVICE
Neutrals always play well together. Try mixing cognac riding boots with black leggings.

4

EMBRACE THE OUTFIT FORMULA

"Alison, I love this concept of outfit formulas, but I'm absolutely, positively convinced that this won't work for me. Sure, it works for everyone else, just not me."

If I had a nickel for every time I've heard this objection...well, I'd have a lot of nickels!

The point is, I hear it a lot.

And I get it. I really, really do.

Way back in the olden days, before Instagram and Pinterest, there was a time in my life when I leisurely leafed through fashion magazines in my spare time on the weekends. I'd see the cutest outfits but would immediately mentally block them from ever appearing on my body. How? By applying my own limiting beliefs about what I could and could not wear.

Now, mind you, no one was telling me I couldn't wear those outfits; this was all a construct created in my own mind about what did and didn't work for me. The worst part was, this way of thinking kept me locked in my comfort zone, so I never even tried to venture out.

I'm not quite sure what happened. But with age, or with knowing myself better, or with no longer caring (as much) what others thought about me, I slowly started to play around with pieces and looks that were previously on the restricted list: white jeans, fun patterns, bright colors, bold accessories, funky shoes, and figure-flattering items. I no longer felt like I had to blend in or camouflage myself to fit in. In fact, even if I didn't leave the house all day, it became downright *fun* to try out new things. My confidence soared!

Along with that realization, something else really important happened—I started to feel *worthy*. Worthy of having fun with my clothes, worthy of feeling confident, worthy of spending a little money and time on myself, worthy of doing what made me feel happy and beautiful.

And it all started with one simple outfit formula.

As I mentioned before, I spent 14 years as a telecom engineer before starting Get Your Pretty On. To say personal style was a departure from that career is a total understatement! Yet when I started down the path of simplifying my wardrobe and creating my first capsule wardrobe, I relied on my engineering skills to "crack the code." Specifically, to create outfit formulas that would work across every style preference, body type, budget, and age. Once I cracked the code, I wanted it to be something that would work for everyone.

HOW THE FIRST OUTFIT FORMULA CAME ABOUT

The first outfit formula I created for myself and the *GYPO* blog consisted of this:

striped top

+ jeans

+ red accessory

+ leopard flats

When I posted my outfit picture and formula on the blog, I was blown away by the response. Dozens of women commented and posted their own photos with their interpretation of the same outfit formula, and eureka! *It. Worked. For. Every. Body.*

No exceptions. Every shape, every budget, every age. Every woman was able to take this simple formula and make it her own by shopping her closet for the pieces, or making substitutions, or buying new items. I was blown away by the women's creativity and the ways they embraced the formula and made it their own. Many of them had fun with the red accessory, pairing it with a red purse, necklace, scarf, or cardigan. Some subbed the leopard flats for red, but all stuck to the striped top and denim bottom pieces of the basic formula.

The beauty of a good outfit formula is that you simply can't mess it up! There's no wrong way to wear it. The Outfit Formulas styling program has proven this over and over. In our private Facebook group, some women wear the formula exactly as it appears, and others take many liberties with it. In general, those who are new to the program tend to follow it to the letter while our veteran Pretties add their own touches to make it their own. Seeing the basic outfit formulas translated by women of so many different shapes, sizes, and demographics is truly one of the most rewarding parts of creating any capsule wardrobe.

> The beauty of a good outfit formula
> is that you simply can't mess it up!
> There's no wrong way to wear it.

As you read through the rest of this book, please keep this in mind. Be open and flexible. Trust the process. If a formula doesn't look like it works for you on the surface, be willing to give it a try. I promise there's a variation of the formula in there that's tailor-made just for you. And by being flexible and creative, you empower yourself to take any fashion style you like and make it your own.

It's your turn: *Do you have the pieces to create the original outfit formula? If so, dive right in and pair it up today, and let me know what you think. Be sure to post it on social media with the hashtag #GYPOOutfitFormulas*

ALISON'S AWESOME ADVICE
By flipping the top and bottom formula prompts, you can easily double your outfit options!

THE GYPO CLOSET CLEAN OUT METHOD

Before we jump into the seasonal outfit formulas chapters, I want to address something *really* important. You may want to skip this, but I encourage you not to because it's going to lay the groundwork for organizing your wardrobe before we add another piece to it.

A few years ago I sent out a survey to *GYPO* readers, asking what the biggest roadblock was to rebuilding their wardrobe. Reason number one was finances, which I totally understand and expected. But the second reason surprised me: Many felt overwhelmed by the current status of their closet. My goal is to help you feel empowered by your closet, not overwhelmed, so I shared my Closet Clean Out method so we could fix this together.

This method was born out of my frustration with my own closet. One of the most frequent requests from *GYPO* readers was for me to do a closet tour. I resisted and resisted because of my dirty little secret—I had a massive amount of closet shame. My own closet was a floor-to-ceiling mess and certainly not one of those Pinterest-worthy closets that other bloggers frequently posted.

After a few years of resistance, I finally decided it was time to change things up, and I enlisted my husband to help. We pulled *everything* out of the closet, one piece at a time. It felt daunting at the time, but honestly, transforming a closet full of clutter and chaos into a clean, organized space is one of the greatest gifts I've ever given to myself.

THE EMOTIONAL TOLL OF YOUR STUFF

We all know that too much stuff can wear us down, but there's another element to cleaning out your closet that we need to address. As you go through this process, you will encounter emotional triggers from sentimental pieces and items that served a past version of yourself. Take time to acknowledge and honor them, and journal your feelings if that's helpful. Remind yourself of the benefits of getting rid of things that no longer serve you. This will help to motivate you and keep you going when the going gets tough and you want to quit.

DEFINE YOUR SPACE

Define your space and use your limits as guidelines. Allow the space you have to determine how much you keep. If you have a small closet, that may mean keeping only a season's worth of clothes at a time in it or reducing the amount of clothing you have. I have a medium-sized closet and keep only one season at a time in it for simplicity and quick decision-making. Do you have a spare room you want to turn into a closet / dressing room? Lucky you! There is no right or wrong—every situation is unique, so use what works for you.

DO THE PREP WORK

Gather up your supplies. You're going to need three large bags or cardboard boxes, a marker, and hangers. (I highly recommend velvet hangers because they don't create shoulder bumps on sweaters, and the velvet clings to even your silkiest camis.) Buy what you think you'll need and save the receipt to return any extras.

Call in reinforcements. Reach out to a friend who will be honest but kind about what looks good and what needs to go. Let them know you are cleaning out your closet and would like their helpful feedback in a few days. This can be done in person or online via text or Facetime. (Bribing with snacks, wine, or chocolate helps! Ask me how I know this.)

Let's do this!

Step One

Pull everything out of your closet. Yes, I said everything. No exceptions. Those concert tees from college wayyyy in the back? You bet your bippy, those too. Take a deep breath and dive in.

You can stack everything on your bed in preparation for the sorting process. Thinking of it like the sorting hat in Harry Potter makes it more fun (at least for me). #gryffindorforlife

Now vacuum out every crevice and wipe down every shelf. Since cleaning isn't fun, let's focus on something that is. Do you want to make your closet prettier? How about adding some paint or a fun wallpaper on one of the walls? Would you like to add some artwork or a mirror? Are there any organizational tools that will make it more functional? Now's the time!

Step Two

Label your boxes or bags Cash, Stash, and Trash. We're going to categorize everything as it comes out of your closet. Here's what to put in each:

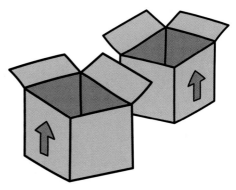

Cash: These are items that can be sold or donated. They are in good condition, but you haven't worn them in a year or more (and let's be honest—you'll probably never wear them again).

Trash: Anything stained, worn out, or damaged beyond repair. My husband generally retrieves these pieces to use for his garage rags.

Stash: This is clothing purgatory. Put anything in here that you haven't worn in two seasons but don't want to part with. This will go into storage, at least for now. Let's call this the "maybe" box.

Step Three

Find a category for each item on your bed (or the sorting hat, as I like to call it), and place it in its respective box. All items that you decide to keep in your wardrobe can be kept on your bed for now.

BUT HOW DO I KNOW WHAT TO KEEP?

That's the million-dollar question, right? Use the following questions as a litmus test:

- Have I worn it in the past year?
- Is it a classic piece that will stay in style?
- Is it still in good condition?
- Can I pair it up in more than one way?
- Do I feel good when I wear this?
- Does it fit?
- Would I buy this again?

If you answered no to one or more of the questions above, it's probably not a keeper. Remember, if it's not a "heck yes," it's a no. You can always put it in the stash box and store it for now. If you're still thinking about it in the next six months, pull it out of the box and use it. If not, tape up the box and donate it.

Pro Tip: As you are sorting, make yourself a Try On pile for the pieces you aren't sure about. If you are an indecisive person, this is where the support system we talked about earlier comes into play. The Get Your Pretty On Pretties Facebook group is also a great place to get kind, honest feedback. You can find a link to it at getyourprettyon.com/book. Try each piece on and acknowledge how it makes you feel. Does the fabric gather in a way that is unflattering and makes you self-conscious? Let it go. Did you instantly place your hand on your hip and feel like you could tackle the world? That's a keeper! If you are still having trouble deciding, take a mirror selfie. Remember, the selfie doesn't lie!

Finally, it's time to put everything in the Keep pile back in your closet. Pull out those beautiful new velvet hangers and start hanging! You can choose any method of organizing that works best for you. I prefer to hang my clothes by type (tanks, tees, short-sleeved blouses, long-sleeved blouses, cardigans, denim jackets, moto jackets, jeans, dress pants, skirts, dresses). You do you and what works best for your space. Some women prefer to sort by color, others by type, some do the KonMari method, and some fold everything. Do what makes the most sense to you while making it easy to pull out pieces and put together outfits.

Were you shocked by how few pieces were in your Keep pile? Don't be—here's why. We only wear about 20 percent of what's in our closet at any given time. So those clothes hanging in there now? That's *your* 20 percent and what you were actually wearing all along. This is a good thing! Now you can confidently fill in the gaps in your wardrobe without being overwhelmed by the unnecessary pieces that were hanging in there that you weren't wearing anyway.

True story: When I did my first closet cleanout, I found 12 black-and-white striped shirts. *Twelve!* I kept buying more because I never took an inventory of what I had or actually needed. On the flip side of that, I cried when I realized how few clothes I actually had (striped shirts notwithstanding) and how far I had to go to have a functional wardrobe. This is totally normal and what this book is designed to help you with. (Lucky you! I didn't have a book.)

> When I did my first closet cleanout, I found 12 black-and-white striped shirts. *Twelve!* I kept buying more because I never took an inventory of what I had or actually needed.

***It's your turn:** You know the routine. Carve out an afternoon this weekend and make the Closet Clean Out happen! And remember, it's going to look worse before it looks better. It's totally normal for your room to look like a bomb went off after emptying your closet. When you're done, pour yourself a glass of champagne or sparkling grape juice (because we fancy like that!) and celebrate. I promise this will be the best gift you give yourself this year. Stand back and admire your work. Now everything in your closet should fit, be in good repair, and make you feel pretty! Cheers to that!*

WARDROBE WORKHORSE: CLOSET STAPLES

If you are rebuilding your wardrobe from scratch or want to know how to prioritize your budget, this is for you! I've mentioned closet staples a few times, but let's dig into what that really means. Closet staples are timeless, classic pieces in your wardrobe. You don't need to worry about them going out of style and can always rely on them as solid foundation pieces to create your outfit formulas.

The majority of closet staple pieces have neutral colors—a white tee, denim jeans, a navy sweater. Since you can count on getting plenty of use from these pieces because they'll be around for the long haul, this is the place to invest in higher-quality items if your budget allows. You'll find lists of seasonal closet staples in the following chapters. Use these lists as your guide when curating your closet, and you'll build a wardrobe that will be fashionable and functional for all seasons for many years to come!

GETTING OUT OF YOUR COMFORT ZONE

I want to take a quick pause here to offer a little reassurance if you're on the verge of panic. If you've spent the last couple of years in a yoga-pants rut like I did, then it's possible that even the idea of wearing a pair of skinny jeans that hugs your curves in all the right places has you feeling just a tad nervous. We all have that one thing (or two or three things) that falls just outside of our comfort zone and makes us feel intimidated...but also kind of excited. Maybe it's wearing leopard print or bold, red lipstick. I've got four tips on how to build your confidence as you take new steps on your style journey.

1. **Start small.** If you love the idea of a leopard-print cardigan but it feels like a little too much for you just yet, start with a lower-risk item. If the cardigan feels too big and bold, try dipping your toe in the leopard-print waters by wearing a leopard-print bracelet or a scarf tied to your purse strap.

2. **Spend small.** The second method of going small is to set a spending limit. We all know what it's like to splurge on a piece of clothing that hangs in our closets and never sees the light of day. With so many other things vying for your hard-earned dollars, your wardrobe is not the place to let money go to waste. If you're intrigued by a certain style but still not 100 percent sold on it, opt for a budget-friendly piece to try out. If you end up wearing it in regular rotation and loving it, then you can feel confident to upgrade to a higher-quality item without the risk that it's going to gather dust in your closet.

3. **Wear it at home.** I'll be totally honest—trying something new can feel awkward and uncomfortable sometimes. No one wants an audience when they are feeling insecure. If you are getting out of your comfort zone by styling something new, wear it around the house. You'll be able to see how it feels, get used to seeing yourself in a new color or cut, and work out any wardrobe malfunctions in the privacy of your own home before you make a public debut.

4. **Take a test run.** Once you're feeling a little more confident in your new style, take it out for a short test run. Wear it to run out and grab some-

thing from the grocery store or to meet up with friends for coffee. This way you get to see how you feel wearing the item in public without being stuck in it the entire day. Nothing is worse than feeling awkward and uncomfortable with no opportunity to change in sight. A quick errand or social visit is a great way to see how you really feel in public with your new look. And remember, confidence is the best accessory, so hold your head high and be proud of yourself for trying something new!

FINDING THE PERFECT WHITE TEE

Finding the perfect white tee can feel like you're hunting a mythical unicorn. Amiright? You'd like to think it exists, but you haven't found it yet. I know this because it's taken me some time to find the perfect white tee and because so many of my readers are still searching. It's one of the top questions asked by *GYPO* readers because it's such a great closet staple. It goes with anything, and it works for all seasons. But why is finding the perfect white tee so hard? It's because we expect a lot from this closet workhorse. We want one that isn't see-through, but it can't be too thick either because it will get most of its use during the spring and summer months.

See? Mythical unicorn.

So where is this elusive white tee? I went straight to the source on this one and asked the fabulous Pretties in my Facebook community. Crowdsourcing seems to work quite nicely on lists like this, and they've never steered me wrong in their recommendations. If you're not in the Pretties Facebook group, I hate to say you're missing out, but you really are. (You can join the Get Your Pretty On Pretties group on Facebook using the link at getyourprettyon.com/book.) The ladies are amazing, and their willingness to help, give advice, and of course, make fantastic recommendations is top-notch! I've listed the white tees our Pretties recommended most often. I love that this list includes shirts for all budgets and all sizes. There's something for everyone, and that's what GYPO is all about.

THE TOP FIVE

1. Land's End

The Pretties' number one choice is the Relaxed Supima White Tee from Land's End. They said it is the perfect thickness and comes in an array of colors and sizes. Sizing options include petite, tall, plus, and petite plus, meaning everyone is sure to find their perfect fit. The tee is available in both crew neck and V-neck options, and they often go on sale with free shipping.

2. Target

Target's A New Day brand received high marks for their Short Sleeve Scoop Neck T-Shirt, their Slim Fit Short Sleeve T-Shirt, and their Slim Fit Short Sleeve V-Neck Fitted T-Shirt. The Pretties said they are the perfect thickness, long enough (hip length), and totally budget-friendly. They are easy to find online or in stores. Also, Target has a great selection of other colors in case you're looking for a great overall tee to add to your closet staples.

3. Amazon Essentials

I have heard this brand mentioned a few times here and there, but I had no idea how truly loved and popular the Amazon Essentials white tees were among the Pretties! They come in an array of colors and in packs of two. They are also available in a crew neck or a V-neck. Pretties stated they are a great thickness, wash up well, and have some stretch to them, which provides a great fit.

4. Eddie Bauer

Eddie Bauer's Favorite Short-Sleeve Crewneck and Favorite Short-

Sleeve V-Neck also received great reviews. Long-sleeve options are available in case you're looking for something for the colder months. They also come in a bunch of different colors and sizes, including petite, plus, and tall. These tees regularly go on sale too.

5. J.Crew Factory

Last but not least among the Pretties (and my) favorites are the white tees from J.Crew Factory. I personally love the Fine-Rib Crewneck Tee, but I know others in the group loved the Girlfriend Crewneck Tee and the Classic Cotton Studio Tee. The Fine-Rib and Girlfriend tees come in a variety of colors, but the Classic Cotton is available only in three colors and is sold out as I'm writing. The Fine-Rib and the Girlfriend, however, are available in sizes that range from XXS to 3X.

6. Honorable Mentions

Although these weren't mentioned as much as the above white tees, they still got some love from our Pretties, so I wanted to include them. Nothing wrong with more recommendations, right?

- Everlane (the Cotton Crew and the Cotton Box-Cut Pocket Tee)
- Old Navy (the Luxe line and the EveryWear line)
- Kohl's (the Sonoma Goods for Life Essential line)
- Madewell
- Target (the Universal Thread line)

TIPS FOR WEARING WHITE TEES

If you find that you're still having trouble finding your perfect tee, here are a few more tips that may help. First, opt for a nude bra or one that is close to your skin color when wearing your white tee. A white bra is more likely to stand out, so a nude bra will blend better and be way less noticeable. Also, make sure you're choosing a white tee that has a great fit. If it's way too tight, it will show everything no matter how thick the fabric is. If that's not what you're looking for, it may be best to size up a bit. Lastly, you can try layering a nude cami under your white tee. This will keep everything looking uniform under your white tee and not see-through.

LET'S TALK COLOR

Adding color to your wardrobe is a great way to elevate your style, but adding the *right* colors to your wardrobe will straight-up knock it out of the park! But how do you know which colors are right for you and which ones to avoid? There are many schools of thought regarding color analysis. Are you a spring or a fall? A cool tone or a warm tone? That's why for this topic I brought in an expert—Samantha Hannah. She has worked as a personal stylist and in the fashion industry for 14 years and is a phenomenal resource on color. Let's explore how to choose the colors that are right for you, and then you can decide whether to take another step and have your own personal color analysis done.

The Color Wheel

Let's take a look at the color wheel and talk about some color basics. Using the image below, we'll begin with the primary colors—red, yellow, and blue. Next we'll consider the secondary colors—green, violet, and orange—which are combinations of two primary colors. Finally we'll look at the intermediate colors, which are created by combining a secondary color with one of its primary colors. For example, yellow plus orange equals yellow-orange.

You can create a lighter tint of a color by adding white to it, or a darker shade by adding black.

Colors that are directly across from each other on the color wheel are called complementary colors. Colors that are slightly to the right and left of the complementary color are called split complementary colors. Finally, any three colors that are side by side on the color wheel are called analogous colors. They can create a harmonious look; however, one of those three colors will tend to dominate.

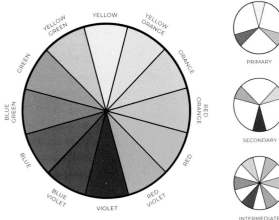

Warm Versus Cool

Colors can be divided into two categories—warm or cool. Warm colors have either a yellow or orange undertone, and cool colors have a blue undertone. For example, a tomato red is a warm red, whereas a raspberry red is a cool red because it has a blue undertone. If you have a cool skin tone, you'll discover that orange is a key color you cannot wear. If you're a warm skin tone, you'll discover you cannot wear baby pink because of its blue undertone. You'll need something closer to a coral shade because of its orangey base. On the color wheel, the cool colors are blue, green, and violet. Red, orange, and yellow are the warm tones.

So, how do you determine whether you're a warm or cool tone? One of the best ways to identify this is with large squares of fabric. Start with the colors orange, icy blue, baby pink, and coral pink. Hold them up against your face in a mirror and note what happens. What colors make you come alive, and what colors make you look unwell? If you're finding it hard to be objective, invite one of your girlfriends over to help you and give you an honest, objective option.

Now it's time to grab a pen and some paper and keep your mirror handy as we dive deeper into how to pick the colors that look the best on you. We're going to focus on three main areas—your eye color, hair color, and skin color.

Eyes

Your eyes are the window to your soul, which is why I like to focus on them first. Begin by writing down your eye color. Now take a closer look at your eyes and describe their color more precisely. Next, look even deeper and identify the other colors in them.

For example, you may start by saying your eyes are blue. After a second look, you may say your eyes are dark blue or light blue. And looking even deeper, you may say you have some amber specs in there or maybe a splash of violet. Is the color deep and rich? Light and bright? Soft and subtle? What did you discover by taking a deeper look at your eyes?

This exercise will instantly show you two colors you can wear with absolute confidence. First is the color of your eyes. By wearing this color, you invite people to look directly into your eyes. The second color is the complementary color to your eye color. For this we're going to use the color wheel again, only this time I chose one that included browns, gray, and black for eye color.

Look on the color wheel and find the color that most closely matches your eyes. Then look directly across from your eye color to find your complementary color. You'll also want to focus on the shade of your eye color. Earlier, we noted whether your eyes were deep and dark, very light, or somewhere in between. Those are the shades on the color wheel you'll want to focus on because they will look best on you. (For the full-color versions of the color wheels shown, please visit getyourprettyon.com/book.)

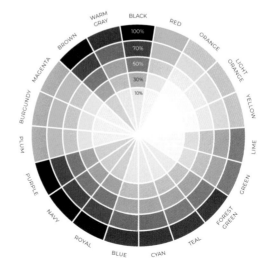

Hair

The next step will involve your hair color. It doesn't matter what your hair color used to be or even your natural color. It really only depends on what your hair color is right now. Describe your hair and look at the overall color. Now look deeper and see what other highlights or lowlights are in your hair. For instance, does your hair have an ashy tone or maybe caramel highlights? Does your hair appear warm or cool? For instance, a natural redhead is warm, and natural white blonds are cool. Once you have this all written down, it's time to move on to your skin tone.

Skin

I know this may sound repetitive, but now it's time to take a look at your skin. What color would you describe your skin? Is your skin color different in summer versus winter? Is there any change? Are you olive or dark? Do you have freckles? What color do your cheeks go when you blush? What color are your lips—are they purply-pink? Rose pink? Dark cherry? Make note of all of this.

Color Contrast Versus Value

Now that you've written out the colors of your eyes, hair, and skin, let's take a step back and look at the whole picture. You don't have to write anything down, but just look at your eyes, hair, and skin as a whole. Do they have a big difference in depth of color? Are they all very deep? Light? Or possibly a mixture of deep and light colors?

Color contrast is the difference in brightness between your eyes, skin, and hair. Someone with high contrast, for example, has dark brown or jet-black hair, bright blue eyes, and very fair skin. Someone with low contrast has hair, skin, and eye color that all sit around the same level. It doesn't matter if that color level is light or dark, only that the hair, skin, and eye color levels are similar.

Color value, on the other hand, is the depth or lightness of your hair, skin, and eyes. Do you appear deep, light, or somewhere in between? The lighter your skin, hair, and eyes, the lighter the colors you can wear. The darker your skin, hair, and eyes, the darker the colors you can wear. Now, here's where it gets tricky (well, trickier). If you find yourself in the middle, meaning you are not overall dark but you are also not overall light, then you'll find that you look great in gray tones as well as neutral and even more muted tones.

WHAT DOES ALL OF THIS MEAN?

Why do we even look at color? Why do women spend money and time year after year on personal color analyses? Because it's not just about color; it's about the placement of that color, and that's what's going to make your eyes come alive and your skin look radiant and leave you feeling fabulous! It's all about the colors you put around your face. If you love coral, but you can't wear it around your face, a cute pair of coral shorts will work. Wearing the right colors that work harmoniously with your hair, skin, and eyes will make you look and feel brighter. Color will affect not only you but also those around you.

I know this was a lot to take in, and you may be reeling a bit. I wanted us to explore the importance and benefits of color, but this just scratches the surface. If you feel this is something worth diving deeper into, I strongly recommend having a color analysis. Many of the ladies in our community and in our Pretties Facebook group have gushed about the impact it had on them and their wardrobe. It's just another piece in the puzzle of having a closet full of clothes you love!

5

DRESSING FOR SPRING

It's time to shake off the dark colors of winter and bloom into spring style! Spring is a time of renewal, and the same should go for your wardrobe. Spring style in my youth included pastels, florals, and nautically inspired pieces. Those trends have carried over to this day and are still some of my favorites.

I also loved the spring dresses I wore as a little girl and will never forget my pink and white polka-dot drop-waist dress that I got for my sister Heather's high school graduation (circa 1989). I was 12 years old, and it was the first dress I wore with pantyhose instead of my little-girl white tights. My mom even let me get a pair of white shoes with a low block heel. I mean, how grown up was that?

Spring is a time of renewal, and the same should go for your wardrobe.

But what if spring style doesn't light you up? Maybe you're more comfortable covering up in those dark-colored clothes, and the bright patterns and colors of spring feel a little too bold for you. If that's the case, then my challenge to you is to add some color and pattern to your spring wardrobe that feels just a little outside your comfort zone.

SPRING STYLE MYTHS AND TRUTHS

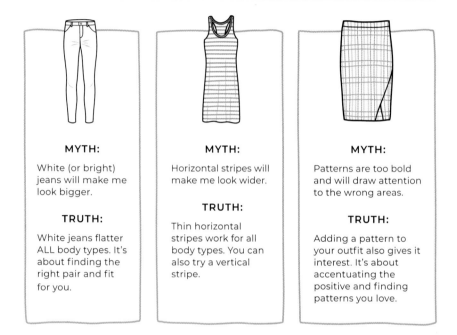

MYTH:

White (or bright) jeans will make me look bigger.

TRUTH:

White jeans flatter ALL body types. It's about finding the right pair and fit for you.

MYTH:

Horizontal stripes will make me look wider.

TRUTH:

Thin horizontal stripes work for all body types. You can also try a vertical stripe.

MYTH:

Patterns are too bold and will draw attention to the wrong areas.

TRUTH:

Adding a pattern to your outfit also gives it interest. It's about accentuating the positive and finding patterns you love.

SPRING COLORS AND CLOSET STAPLE ESSENTIALS

Lighten up, Buttercup! We see spring's color palette in nature, from pastels, like light pink and lavender, to bolder Kelly green and bright pink and yellow. It's a time for blooming and rebirth, and your style should be no exception. Is there a new piece you've wanted to add to your spring wardrobe?

Here's a list of some closet staple essentials that will last for many springs to come.

GRAY TEE

STRIPED TOP

FLORAL TOP

CHAMBRAY BUTTON-DOWN

WHITE TANK

WHITE TEE

WHITE JEANS

COLORED DENIM

BOYFRIEND JEANS

GRAY JEANS

DARK-WASH JEANS

DENIM JACKET

UTILITY JACKET

FLORAL DRESS

NEUTRAL CARDIGANS

BRIGHT CARDIGAN

SPRING SHOPPING LIST

With the items on this shopping list, you'll be able to create any of the spring outfit formulas that follow. Don't forget to shop your closet first, and always choose shoes that are functional for your lifestyle.

TOPS

Striped	☐
Gray	☐
Floral/Printed	☐
Chambray Shirt	☐
White Tee	☐
Graphic Sweatshirt	☐
White Tank Top	☐
Printed Blouse	☐

DRESSES

Shirt Dress	☐
Floral Dress	☐
Solid Sheath Dress	☐

BOTTOMS

Can be jeans, skirts, shorts or pants.

Light Wash Denim	☐
Medium Wash Denim	☐
Dark Wash Denim	☐
Boyfriend Jeans	☐
White	☐
Olive	☐

FOOTWEAR

Choose the type of footwear that works best for your lifestyle.

Metallic	☐
Leopard	☐
Bright	☐
Neutral	☐
Taupe Ankle Boots	☐
White Sneakers	☐

LAYERS

Dark Neutral Cardigan	☐
Light Neutral Cardigan	☐
Utility Jacket	☐
Bright Cardigan	☐
Trench Coat	☐
Denim Jacket	☐
Moto Jacket or Blazer	☐

ACCESSORIES

Hoop Earrings	☐
Printed Hair Scarf	☐
Statement Necklace	☐
Delicate Short Necklace	☐
Printed Scarf	☐
Stud Earrings	☐
Statement Earrings	☐
Pendant Necklace	☐
Neutral Drop Earrings	☐

For a printable version of this shopping list that you can check off, visit getyourprettyon.com/book.

I asked hundreds of GYPO Pretties to share their all-time favorite spring outfit formulas. Check out their top three choices and what they had to say.

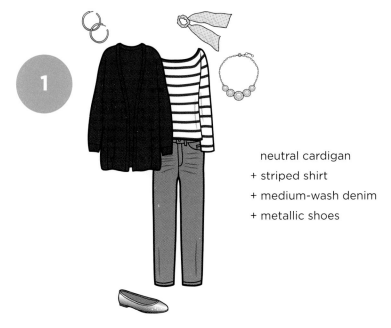

neutral cardigan
+ striped shirt
+ medium-wash denim
+ metallic shoes

"It is simple and classic and easily adapted to changing temperatures." —Dandy L. (age 50)

"This outfit is comfortable, casual, and chic. I can run errands or head out for date night. Love it!" —Kim D. (age 53)

"I love a classic pair of jeans, and adding stripes is always a good thing! I feel like this outfit is appropriate for so many things and is still comfortable." —Shannon F. (age 38)

2

utility jacket
+ gray tee
+ medium-wash denim
+ metallic shoes

"It's super casual and comfortable for a work-at-home mama like me."
—Tara H. (age 45)

"It's so simple, and most people probably already have the individual pieces in their closet, but when you add something a little bit unexpected—like a metallic shoe—it really starts to feel intentional." —Angela P. (age 45)

"I like that it's simple and comfortable but still makes me feel put together. It's a combination I wouldn't have tried on my own." —LeDawn K. (age 43)

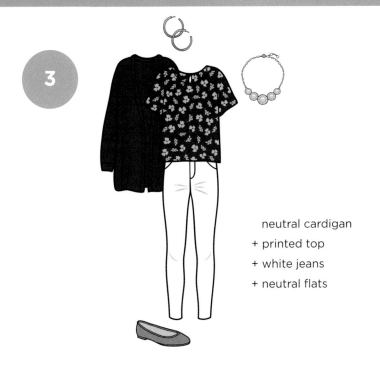

3

neutral cardigan
+ printed top
+ white jeans
+ neutral flats

"The contrast between the white bottoms and the dark floral top, and the long line of the sweater—that's a formula that *always* works for me." —Deb G. (age 57)

"Feminine with bright colors and contrast with the white jeans, but not too dressy for an average day of errands and appointments." —Jaime W. (age 41)

"I love white jeans! I've been so surprised how great they look on women of all different sizes and shapes. This outfit is nice enough to wear out to a brunch but also to the PTA meeting. I love a slightly elevated jeans and T-shirt look!" —Krista H. (age 39)

bright cardigan
+ striped top
+ dark-wash denim
+ leopard shoes

chambray shirt
+ striped top
+ white jeans
+ leopard shoes

neutral cardigan

+ white tee

+ boyfriend denim

+ taupe ankle boots

+ printed scarf

utility jacket

+ graphic sweatshirt

+ light-wash denim

+ sneakers

trench coat
+ shirt dress
+ neutral wedges

denim jacket
+ gray tee
+ white jeans
+ taupe ankle boots
+ printed scarf

I've always had a thing for all white. The chambray button-down shirt and metallic sandals add just the right amount of detail to this easy laid-back look. Add accessories as you please. (Psst—a bright purse would look awesome with this!)

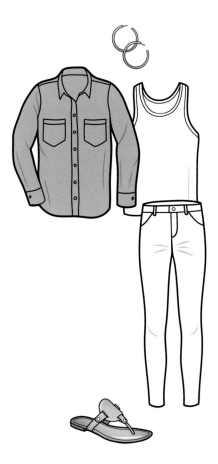

chambray shirt
+ white tank top
+ white jeans
+ metallic sandals

At the heart of it all, I'm just a T-shirt and jeans kind of girl. I love the slouchiness of a gray tee half tucked into the front of boyfriend jeans with some comfy kicks. Nothing says "cool mom" style quite like it.

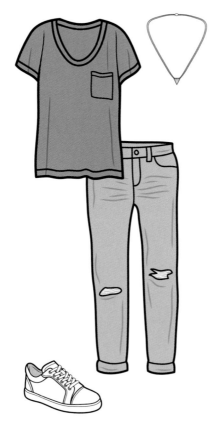

gray tee

+ boyfriend jeans

+ white sneakers

Stripes, white jeans, and an Audrey Hepburn vibe...what's not to love? This classic outfit formula will never go out of style, especially when topped with a perennially stylish trench coat.

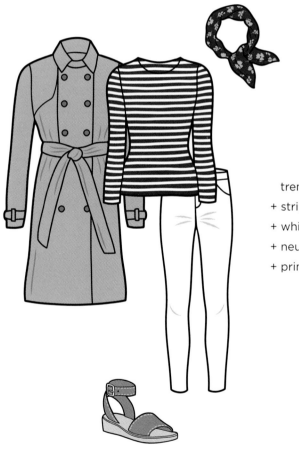

trench coat
+ striped top
+ white jeans
+ neutral sandals
+ printed scarf

Spring is filled with a lot of special events, from Easter Sunday to graduation ceremonies. There can be a lot of pressure to find the right outfit that will live in infamy in photos online. Here are my top three spring special occasion outfits:

trench coat + floral dress + neutral sandals

"Elegance is
the only beauty
that never fades."

—AUDREY HEPBURN

moto jacket or blazer + sheath dress + neutral heels

As the weather warms up, keep your makeup to a minimum and swipe on a bright red lip for the ultimate accessory.

shirt dress + bright shoes

Printed blouses are a closet workhorse. If you find a style you like, buy it in a few different patterns and apply the same basic outfit formula.

denim jacket + printed blouse + white jeans + neutral shoes

neutral cardigan + floral top + olive jeans + neutral sandals

black moto jacket + striped top + boyfriend jeans + bright heels

Bonus—Tips for Picking the Perfect Pair of White Jeans

Ah, white jeans—possibly the most polarizing of any piece in the history of outfit formulas. The funny thing is, once I twist your arm hard enough to convince you to try them and you finally find the perfect pair, you're all #whitejeansforlife. It's truly a beautiful thing! Believe me when I say that a great-fitting pair of white jeans is every bit as flattering as any other color. If you tend to want to wear darker colors on bottom to downplay your...er, assets, then I'm going to work extra hard on you. I too used to employ this technique, and while yes, it is true, I can assure you that wearing white does not magically make you appear to be two sizes bigger. It's all about the perfect fit, finding a pair with just the right amount of stretch, and never giving up until you succeed at your mission.

Follow these five tips to ensure your success:

1. Use your body shape as your guide. Try on pairs that are recommended for your unique shape.
2. Look for a pair with a little bit of stretch. This is really key to them fitting well and flattering *every* body type.
3. Thicker denim fabrics are more flattering and will show fewer lumps and bumps.
4. Try to find a pair with nude colored pockets and wear nude-colored undergarments, not white.
5. Bleach your white jeans every few washes to keep them bright. Carry a Tide To Go Pen in your purse for (inevitable) mishaps.

6

DRESSING FOR SUMMER

Oh, summer! You tend to trip us up more than any other time of the year by taunting us with your warmer weather and exposed body parts. Even if we make it through spring unscathed, summer is waiting with its skimpier styles, bathing suits, shorts, and sleeveless tops that can do a number on our self-esteem.

One of the biggest objections I constantly hear from GYPO Pretties is that they can't wear (fill in the blank). And here, my friend, is where I step in to say yes, you can. I'm going to repeat it in case you're saying no, no, not me. *Yes, you can!*

I have a personal story to share, one of a beautiful woman (the most beautiful woman I've ever seen) who had these limitations. I've never seen her wear a pair of shorts or a sleeveless top, and I've seen her in a bathing suit only a handful of times in her entire life. Her wardrobe consists of all dark-colored pants, and she hasn't worn jeans for many years. The limitations she's placed on herself held her back from so many things. She's never gone to the pool or traveled abroad (although this was always a dream of hers). She allowed these insecurities to keep her from attending events and being visible, even when it meant missing out on something meaningful.

That woman is my mother.

And although I haven't shared this story anywhere publicly, she *is* the reason why I do what I do. Maybe it's a form of therapy for me. As a little girl, seeing my mother struggle so much with her body image hurt me deeply. I wanted nothing more than for her to accept herself for how God created her and to live her life fully. When I looked at her, I didn't see the flaws that she did—just a beautiful woman who deserved to be happy and live a vibrant, full life. It affected me deeply on many levels.

When a woman shares with me that she wore (fill in the blank) for the first time and felt confident because of GYPO, I get this validation that I'm doing the right thing. Nothing brings me more joy than hearing from a reader that she tried something totally outside her comfort zone and felt like a million bucks.

> As a little girl, seeing my mother struggle so much with her body image hurt me deeply. I wanted nothing more than for her to accept herself for how God created her and to live her life fully.

Through the years of doing the outfit formulas program, I've heard from countless women who've said that it was a springboard for many other changes in their lives—embarking on a healthier lifestyle, going back to school, taking a bucket-list trip, changing careers...you name it! One simple change kicked off a chain reaction of confidence in all other areas of life.

During the summer months, my challenge to you is to celebrate your body, no matter what shape or type you have. Wear the shorts, try the color that you thought you'd never wear, put on the sleeveless top, wear the bikini, and be brave and bold with your patterns. YOLO, right?

SUMMER STYLE MYTHS AND TRUTHS

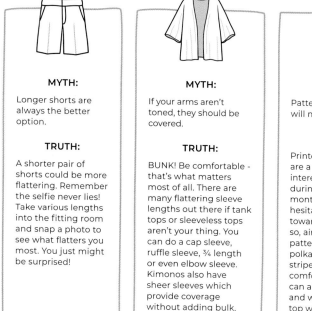

MYTH:

Longer shorts are always the better option.

TRUTH:

A shorter pair of shorts could be more flattering. Remember the selfie never lies! Take various lengths into the fitting room and snap a photo to see what flatters you most. You just might be surprised!

MYTH:

If your arms aren't toned, they should be covered.

TRUTH:

BUNK! Be comfortable - that's what matters most of all. There are many flattering sleeve lengths out there if tank tops or sleeveless tops aren't your thing. You can do a cap sleeve, ruffle sleeve, ¾ length or even elbow sleeve. Kimonos also have sheer sleeves which provide coverage without adding bulk.

MYTH:

Patterns on my lower body will make me look bigger.

TRUTH:

Printed shorts and skirts are a fun way to add interest to your outfit during hot summer months. But you may be hesitant to draw the eye toward your lower half. If so, aim for smaller scale patterns like ditzy florals, polka dots or vertical stripes. If you're still not comfortable though, you can always "flip the script" and wear the pattern on top with a solid bottom.

SUMMER COLORS AND CLOSET STAPLE ESSENTIALS

The summer color palette takes its inspiration from your favorite beach vacation. Bold blues and soft aquas, sun-washed colors, bright whites and coral...just to name a few. Picture that tropical cocktail melting in your hand and capture the colors that go along with it!

Here is a list of closet staple essentials for summer:

GRAY TEE   STRIPED TOP   WHITE TANK AND TEE

STRIPED TANKS AND TEES   BRIGHT TANKS AND TEES

PATTERNED KIMONOS   DENIM JACKET AND/OR CHAMBRAY SHIRT

MAXI DRESSES

TANK DRESSES

SHORT TANK OR TEE DRESSES

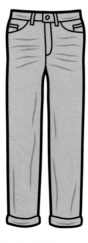

DENIM SHORTS OR JEANS

WHITE SHORTS OR PANTS

HOW TO ADD INTEREST WITHOUT ADDING HEAT

One of the biggest questions I get asked during the summer months is, "How can I keep my outfits interesting in the summer without adding layers and heat?" It's an awesome question, says the woman who lives in tank tops, shorts, and flip-flops in the sweltering Texas heat. Honestly, it took me a few years to figure it out, but here's a list of surefire ways to add panache to your summer uniform without having to drink extra Gatorade.

1. **Kimonos.** I love me some kimonos and try to put one on every summer shopping list. Why? They're a lightweight layer that adds *tons* of visual interest, pattern, and detail to an outfit without layering on warmth. Look for one in a sheer fabric to allow the summer breeze to pass through.

2. **Colorful necklaces.** A bright beaded necklace goes a long way toward adding style to your outfit. Pair up a basic solid tee or tank in one of the colors of the necklace with some white shorts or jeans and sandals for an instant outfit.

3. **Statement earrings.** Just like beaded necklaces, statement earrings are another way to add details to your look without adding heat. Pull your hair up to keep it cool and allow your earrings to be the star of the show!

4. **Printed and colorful shoes.** This is the time of the year to have fun with your footwear! Printed and colorful shoes, particularly sandals, add personality to your outfits and can be a great outfit starter. Just pull out your favorite pair and partner them with pieces in your wardrobe that coordinate.

SUMMER SHOPPING LIST

With the items on this shopping list, you'll be able to create any of the summer outfit formulas that follow. Don't forget to shop your closet first, and always choose shoes that are functional for your lifestyle.

TOPS

White ☐
Navy ☐
Striped ☐
Bright ☐
Chambray ☐
Printed ☐
Gray ☐
Blue/White Striped ☐

BOTTOMS

Can be jeans, skirts, shorts or pants.

Denim ☐
White ☐
Printed ☐

LAYERS

Kimono ☐
Denim Jacket ☐
White Denim Jacket ☐

DRESSES

Solid Dress or Jumpsuit ☐
Printed Maxi Dress or Jumpsuit ☐
Solid Sheath Dress ☐

FOOTWEAR

Choose the type of footwear that works best for your lifestyle.

Neutral ☐
Bright ☐
Leopard ☐
Metallic ☐

ACCESSORIES

Hoop Earrings ☐
Pendant Necklace ☐
Delicate Short Necklace ☐
Statement Earrings ☐
Clutch Purse ☐
Stud Earrings ☐

For a printable version of this shopping list you can check off, visit getyourprettyon.com/book.

I asked hundreds of GYPO Pretties to share their all-time favorite summer outfit formulas. Check out their top three choices and what they had to say.

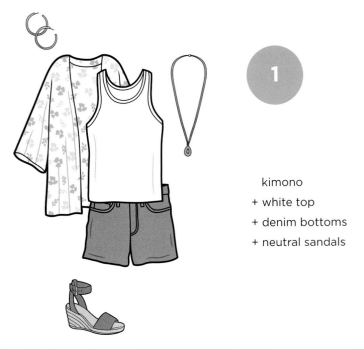

kimono
+ white top
+ denim bottoms
+ neutral sandals

"I love the kimono because it's lightweight but still covers my arms."
—Anya Y. (age 39)

"I love how a white tee and denim shorts get a whole new look with a colorful kimono and accessories. I also love the variety of textures this outfit has." —Nicole M. (age 34)

"I received random compliments from strangers wearing that outfit!"
—Beth F. (age 62)

2

white top
+ denim bottoms
+ bright sandals

"It is feminine and has a pop of color, but it's a great mix of closet staples that can go with loads of other things." —Jennifer A. (age 43)

"Who doesn't already have a white tee and denim shorts? Like so many of Alison's formulas, this one takes pieces you already have and shows how to add trendy accessories to update and personalize the look." —Carolyn J. (age 68)

"It's a simple classic with a pop of color—perfect for summer. How can you go wrong?" —Lynnette T. (age 44)

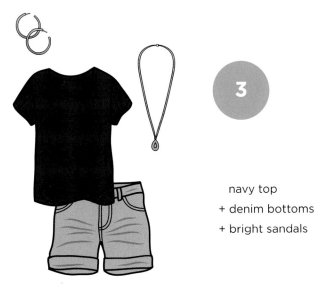

3

navy top
+ denim bottoms
+ bright sandals

"A T-shirt and shorts feels practical for life in the summer, but when you elevate it with cute sandals and nice accessories, you can be pretty *and* practical." —Andrea L. (age 39)

"It's casual yet cute! The shoes and necklace take simple jeans and a tee to a new level. I also love that there is a little detail on the T-shirt." —Pam H. (age 49)

"It's cute. You can easily replicate it with items from your closet or get these on a budget." —Kristi M. (age 47)

solid dress
or jumpsuit
+ leopard shoes

denim jacket
+ striped top
+ white shorts
+ metallic shoes

bright top
+ printed bottoms
+ metallic shoes

white denim jacket
+ printed maxi dress
+ bright shoes

chambray shirt
+ white tee or tank
+ white shorts
+ bright shoes

printed top
+ denim shorts
+ metallic shoes

I love the casual yet classic vibe of this pairing. It also works with white shorts or a chambray shirt instead of the denim jacket.

denim jacket
+ gray tee
+ white jeans
+ metallic sandals

Sometimes I have just one outfit formula in mind when I start to create a capsule wardrobe—this was one of those special ones that inspired a whole season. A lightweight blue and white striped top are the perfect way to usher in summer.

striped top
+ white shorts
+ bright sandals

This is my go-to summer travel outfit. The maxi dress ensures that it's as comfy as my favorite pajamas. I usually add a tie-front chambray shirt to take the chill off in the plane, and some slip-on (and off) metallic sandals make it a breeze to get through security.

Did you know that a chambray shirt makes a great top layer for your summer outfits? Try knotting one at the bottom and wearing it in place of a heavier denim jacket!

maxi dress
+ chambray shirt
+ metallic sandals

Weddings, Fourth of July picnics, summer vacations...some of the best occasions of the year happen in the summer!

denim jacket
+ gray top
+ white shorts
+ bright shoes

printed maxi dress or jumpsuit + neutral wedges

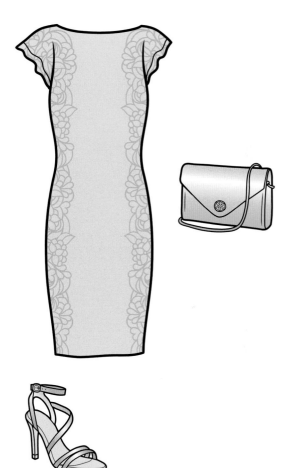

sheath dress + metallic heels + clutch

white denim jacket + printed top + denim shorts + neutral shoes

blue or white top + printed shorts + neutral shoes

denim jacket + printed top + white shorts + neutral shoes

Bonus—How to Create the Perfect Packing List

Learn how to pack like a pro with this easy process. I've taught this to all three of my kids, and they've been packing for vacations by themselves since they were old enough to zip a suitcase—how awesome is that? I promise, once you learn this process, you'll never dread packing again. Yes, that's a *big* promise, but I'm confident enough to say you can go ahead and get your thank-you letter ready for me now.

8 Steps to Perfect Packing

1. Write out a clothing itinerary for each day of your trip. For example, on day one you may write down "travel day" so you know how to dress accordingly. Day two could be "sightseeing, beach day, and dinner out." Whatever your day entails, write down those activities.

2. Using your outfit itinerary as a guide, choose some of your favorite bottoms, tops, dresses, shoes, and accessories from your seasonal wardrobe that will be appropriate for your daily activities. You'll want to start with at least three pairs of bottoms, three or four tops, a dress, and two or three pairs of shoes. It's perfectly fine to start with more and then curate down as you work through the process. These numbers will also vary depending upon how long your trip is and whether laundry facilities will be available. Obviously, a four-day weekend requires a lot less than a long European tour!

Need a packing list for your upcoming vacation? Be sure to check out the resources at getyourprettyon.com/book for done-for-you packing lists for all kinds of trips!

3. Lay one of the bottoms on your floor or bed. Or start with a dress if you'd prefer.

4. Combine this first pair of bottoms with a top, shoes, and accessories from the other pieces you've pulled out. Take a photo with your phone of this outfit pairing.

5. Repeat creating pairings until your bottoms (or dress) are used two or three times.

6. Move on to the next pair of bottoms and repeat the process. Pair up your tops and footwear in at least two or three ways if possible.

7. Once you've created all the pairings you need for your trip, reassess the pieces you pulled out to see if you need to add in an extra outfit, just to be safe, or if you can eliminate any of them.

8. Pack your bags and enjoy your vacation! Refer back to the photos on your phone for your daily outfit inspiration.

Swimwear a struggle? You can't go wrong with a classic black one-piece, tankini, or bikini! Head to the fitting room of your favorite department store with several styles in solid black to find your perfect fit. Be sure to complete your look with a cute pool cover-up (did somebody say leopard print?) for an ultra-chic beachy vibe!

7

DRESSING FOR FALL

Fall signals the return of layers and textures to your wardrobe. It's also a great time to reevaluate your wardrobe for any gaps you may need to fill. You'll generally wear your fall clothes through the winter months, so you can safely add some investment pieces if needed.

I created one of my all-time favorite fall outfit formulas at the age of 14. That year I bought a gorgeous chunky cable-knit ivory sweater and paired it with navy dress pants, cognac penny loafers, and a printed paisley scarf with hues of burgundy, olive, navy, and cream. The funny thing is, this classic outfit formula would be just as stylish today, more than 30 years later. Was I a teenage style psychic? No, it's just proof that if you stick with the classics, you'll never, ever go wrong!

FALL COLORS AND CLOSET STAPLE ESSENTIALS

Ochre, burgundy, navy, mustard, deep garnet, peacock green, rust, teal, dusty mauve—oh, the colors of fall. Be still, my heart! So many beautiful colors inspired by the changing landscape around us. (Unless you live in Texas like me. Then you just get brown and light brown.)

Here is a list of closet staple essentials for fall:

> "Character. Intelligence. Strength. Style. That makes beauty."
>
> **—DIANE VON FURSTENBERG**

STRIPED TOP

CHAMBRAY SHIRT

PRINTED OR FLORAL TOP

NEUTRAL SWEATERS

GRAY JEANS

BLACK JEANS

DARK-WASH JEANS

DENIM JACKET

NEUTRAL CARDIGANS

UTILITY JACKET

FALL STYLE MYTHS AND TRUTHS

MYTH:

You can't wear white jeans after Labor Day.

TRUTH:

Oh yes you can! Don't pack your white jeans away after summer. You can continue to pair them up with fall's neutrals like gray and taupe or any hue in the fall color palette.

MYTH:

Button down shirts aren't for big busted women.

TRUTH:

Fall signals a return to layering and button down shirts are a great piece for this. If you're larger busted though, you may experience gapping in your buttons. Size up on your button down to fit your chest and don't be afraid to invest a few dollars into some tailoring to get the right fit everywhere else.

MYTH:

Scarves add bulk to an outfit.

TRUTH:

Not all scarves are created equal. If bulky scarves aren't your thing, look for fall patterns in lightweight fabrics like polyester blends. You can still add pattern and interest to your outfit without adding bulk or weight.

FALL SHOPPING LIST

With the items on this shopping list, you'll be able to create any of the fall outfit formulas that follow. Don't forget to shop your closet first, and always choose shoes that are functional for your lifestyle.

TOPS

Navy ☐
Bright ☐
Striped ☐
Solid ☐
White ☐
Chambray Shirt ☐
White Button Down ☐
Gray Sweatshirt ☐

BOTTOMS

Can be jeans, skirts, shorts or pants.

Gray ☐
Burgundy ☐
Black ☐
Olive ☐
Dark Wash Jeans ☐
Boyfriend Jeans ☐

LAYERS

Blazer ☐
Denim Jacket ☐
Neutral Cardigan ☐
Utility Jacket ☐
Moto Jacket ☐

DRESSES

Printed Dress ☐
Solid Dress ☐

FOOTWEAR

Choose the type of footwear that works best for your lifestyle.

Taupe Ankle Boots ☐
Blank Ankle Boots ☐
Leopard ☐
Bright ☐
Metallic ☐
Riding Boots ☐
Black Tall Boots ☐

ACCESSORIES

Hoop Earrings ☐
Floral/Printed Scarf ☐
Pendant Necklace ☐
Short Delicate Necklace ☐
Stud Earrings ☐
Plaid Scarf ☐
Statement Earrings ☐

For a printable version of this shopping list that you can check off, visit getyourprettyon.com/book.

I asked hundreds of GYPO Pretties to share their all-time favorite fall outfit formulas. Check out their top three choices and what they had to say.

1

floral scarf
+ navy sweater
+ gray jeans
+ taupe booties

"I love navy, and this scarf softens the look while elevating it at the same time!" —Alexis C. (age 43)

"This was something I didn't expect to love as much as I did, but I got so many compliments on how effortlessly put together I looked!" —Laura L. (age 47)

"This is one of those outfits that I can wear to work or on a day off and feel great! The navy boatneck sweater and gray jeans are so good together, and the scarf really gives it some pop!" —Lisa O. (age 51)

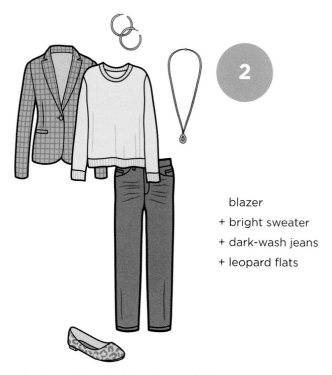

blazer
+ bright sweater
+ dark-wash jeans
+ leopard flats

"The pop of color with a traditional tweed blazer adds a contemporary fun feeling to this classic outfit. The leopard shoes are unexpected and fun!" —Cheryl K. (age 52)

"Fall always seems like it should be a little preppy, and I liked the color choices for this one." —Stephanie F. (age 51)

"A pop of color is hanging on to summer just a little longer. I love these colors as they are 'fallish.' Paired with dark pants, this is a killer good outfit. The icing on the cake is animal print on your shoes." —Tammy T. (age 56)

3

denim jacket
+ striped top
+ burgundy jeans
+ leopard flats

"Everything I love in one outfit. Because of GYPO I have learned how to put together outfits using a simple formula that includes stripes and leopard!" —Cheryl C. (age 52)

"I love these pants for fall and the use of classic closet staples—jean jacket and striped tee—that most women already have." —Mary Ellen S. (age 43)

"Leopard and stripes :) Need I say more?" —Laurie C. (age 45)

Striped shirts never, ever go out of style. They're a perennial fall staple that adds a little polish to any outfit.

denim jacket
+ striped top
+ gray jeans
+ bright shoes

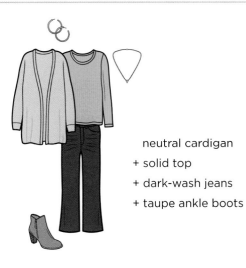

neutral cardigan
+ solid top
+ dark-wash jeans
+ taupe ankle boots

denim jacket
+ printed dress
+ bright shoes

neutral cardigan
+ chambray shirt
+ gray jeans
+ black ankle boots

blazer
+ white button-down
+ boyfriend jeans
+ leopard shoes

gray sweatshirt
+ printed scarf
+ boyfriend jeans
+ metallic shoes

Want to know a secret? This is my favorite outfit formula I've ever created. There's just something so classic about it. The riding boots, chambray shirt, and cardigan with a plaid scarf are absolute perfection.

plaid scarf
+ neutral cardigan
+ chambray shirt
+ black jeans
+ riding boots

Pattern mixing is one of my favorite trends to incorporate into an outfit formula. The subtle pattern mix of a floral scarf and striped shirt in this outfit makes it ideal to try the trend without feeling too daring.

printed scarf
+ utility jacket
+ striped top
+ black jeans
+ ankle boots

My moto jacket and a white tee are the two pieces I wear most in fall. Throw on a chic printed scarf to complete this look.

Cuff the bottom of your pants or jeans to show a tiny bit of ankle above your ankle boots.

printed scarf

+ moto jacket

+ white tee

+ gray jeans

+ taupe ankle boots

From hayrides with the kids to holiday family portraits, fall is full of fun family times and memories to be made.

neutral cardigan + solid dress + riding boots + printed scarf

denim jacket + printed dress + ankle boots

neutral cardigan + chambray shirt + black jeans + plaid scarf
+ taupe ankle boots

Family Portraits

Fall is the time of year when we try to fit family portraits into our schedules. I know it sounds simple, but the task of pulling off a perfectly executed family picture can be a bit daunting. Whether it's something we do every year or every five-plus years, the first question that comes to mind is usually what to wear. I love family photos where the theme is effortless style. Every outfit coordinates but is not too matchy-matchy, and everyone is able to wear colors and clothes that they feel confident in and that look great on them. This comfort and confidence translates into a fun, beautiful family photo that you can't wait to show off. I can't help with making everyone smile at the camera at the same time, but I can help with some fall family photo outfit ideas.

1. Ladies First

I must insist that you pick your outfit first! Find an outfit that you feel amazing in and colors you love, and build off that. Finding clothes that we like and that fit well can be hard enough, but then to put limitations on ourselves because we already found clothes for the rest of the family just adds unnecessary pressure.

2. Shop Your Closet First

You may be surprised to discover that you already have coordinating outfits for the family and didn't even know it. Take the time to look through everyone's closet first and see what items you have in the same color family. In the end, you may find out you need to add only a few pieces to pull everything together instead of purchasing everyone a new head-to-toe look.

3. Shop Collections

If new outfits for the little ones are a must, shop a company or store that carries kids' clothing collections. It will help take some of the guesswork out of shopping for the little ones and will ensure that the colors coordinate. Plus, getting everything in one place is always a bonus.

4. Neutral Is Not Boring

Using a neutral color palette is not boring if done right. Adding layers and texture through jackets, scarves, and accessories will add dimension to your fall family photo. Also, be sure to vary your neutral color palette. Make sure your creams, whites, grays and other neutrals are a few shades off. If the color is too similar, everyone will blend, and your photo will lack depth.

5. Don't Be Afraid of Color

Fall brings some of the most beautiful colors, so take advantage of the season. Be sure to choose colors that compliment your skin tone and hair color and won't make you look washed out in your photos. Colors should enhance but not take over. Also, consider where in your home you plan to display your family photo. Would the colors in your photo work with the decor in your home? Lastly, consider where your photos will be taken. Remember that colors may look different under artificial light than they will outside. When planning your outfits and colors, use natural light before making a final decision, and consider what colors will be in your background.

moto jacket + printed dress + black boots

solid blouse + olive jeans + taupe ankle boots

printed scarf + moto jacket + solid tee + dark-wash jeans
+ taupe ankle boots

Bonus—Maximize Your Budget: Investment Items and How to Keep Your Look Fresh

Since fall is the perfect time to add some classic basics, you may be in the market for some investment items that will last for years to come. You know I'm all about more bang for your buck! Follow these three rules to know where to invest your clothing budget.

1. **Calculate a cost-per-wear basis.** When you're buying investment items, think about how often you'll wear them. You may want to invest in higher-quality pieces when it comes to items like coats, handbags, boots, and shoes. These are pieces you're going to wear season after season for years to come. You'll want these pieces to wear well. When in doubt, estimate how often you'll wear a piece and calculate it over the amount of time. (Wait—I promised earlier that there wouldn't be more math in this book. Well, I lied! This math is an awesome justification for shopping.) Think about it, if you buy the $50 purse every season that you carry for only three months, would it make more sense to spend a few hundred dollars on a better-quality version that you can carry for years to come? Same goes for shoes and boots. Invest in classics, and you may actually *save*!

   Which brings me to...

2. **Invest in classic basics—not trends.** Trends come and go, so reserve the majority of your budget for pieces that stand the test of time.

3. **Incorporate budget-friendly seasonal trends.** Pick up a few fun finds to keep things fresh each season. Add a patterned blouse, a pretty scarf, an animal print, the latest color trend, or some on-trend accessories to jazz up your basics.

DRESSING FOR WINTER

It's time to bundle up! Layer on the warmth and add in some plaid, faux fur, and velvet. Winter is all about sumptuous, cozy style in fabrics that make you feel like you're floating in a cloud of marshmallows on a warm mug of hot cocoa.

But don't forget the sparkle! With Christmas and New Year's on the docket during the winter months, there are plenty of opportunities to add a little bling to brighten the darkest days of winter.

WINTER COLORS AND CLOSET STAPLE ESSENTIALS

Winter's color palette is often dominated by darker colors, but there's certainly been a shift to "anything goes" over the past few years. Colors from soft pastels to jewel tones and even bright pinks and greens are totally on-trend and offer a fun way to play around with color in what can otherwise be a bleak time of the year, depending on where you live.

Here's a list of closet staple essentials for winter:

ALISON'S AWESOME ADVICE

Fit is absolutely key. Don't buy your clothes too big or too small, and don't be afraid to have even inexpensive pieces tailored to fit better.

LONG-SLEEVED LAYERING TEES

NEUTRAL SWEATERS

STRIPED TOP

CHAMBRAY SHIRT

SOLID BLOUSES

PLAID BUTTON-DOWN

BLACK TURTLENECK

GRAY JEANS

BLACK JEANS

DARK-WASH JEANS

SWEATER DRESS   PUFFER JACKET   WOOL COAT

WINTER STYLE MYTHS AND TRUTHS

MYTH:

Adding faux fur pieces will make me look like a Yeti.

TRUTH:

A little dash of faux fur can add elegance to any look. Try it out in more subtle ways with a faux fur scarf, the lining of the hood on your coat or a faux fur collar on a quilted vest. You can always work your way up to all over faux fur pieces like vests and jackets.

MYTH:

Plaid shirts are for lumberjacks.

TRUTH:

Umm, stylish lumberjacks! But seriously, I get it. Plaid shirts can conjure up images of the Brawny paper towel guy but they can also be a stylish way to add pattern to your outfit. Try one with a statement necklace for a dash of sophistication. Take that lumberjack!

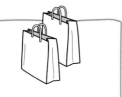

MYTH:

Winter events are stressful and require shopping for new outfits for all of them.

TRUTH:

You can easily shop your closet and dress up your staples! If in doubt, all black is always a good idea. Try pairing up a black blouse with black ankle pants or a pencil skirt or pull out your favorite LBD and embellish it with some statement making jewelry. Just add heels and voila! Instant party outfit.

WINTER SHOPPING LIST

With the items on this shopping list, you'll be able to create any of the winter outfit formulas that follow. Don't forget to shop your closet first, and always choose shoes that are functional for your lifestyle.

TOPS

Black Turtleneck ☐
Gray Turtleneck ☐
Striped ☐
Graphic Sweatshirt ☐
Plaid Shirt ☐
Chambray Shirt ☐
Neutral Sweater ☐
Solid Sweater ☐
Neutral Tunic ☐
Solid Tunic ☐
Solid Blouse ☐
Black Blouse ☐
Black Sweater ☐

BOTTOMS

Can be jeans, skirts, or pants.

Black (Velvet Optional) ☐
Gray ☐
Burgundy ☐
Dark Wash Jeans ☐
Black Leggings ☐
Plaid ☐

LAYERS

Neutral Vest ☐
Black Jacket ☐
Neutral Wool Coat ☐
Neutral Cardigan ☐
Faux Fur Vest ☐
Faux Fur Coat ☐

DRESSES

Solid Sweater Dress ☐
Plaid Sheath Dress ☐

FOOTWEAR

Choose the type of footwear that works best for your lifestyle.

Leopard ☐
Black ☐
White Sneakers ☐
Black Ankle Boots ☐
Riding Boots ☐
Rugged Boots ☐

ACCESSORIES

Hoop Earrings ☐
Buffalo Plaid Scarf ☐
Black Tights ☐
Delicate Short Necklace ☐
Plaid/Printed Scarf ☐
Pendant Necklace ☐
Statement Earrings ☐
Statement Necklace ☐

For a printable version of this shopping list that you can check off, visit getyourprettyon.com/book.

I asked hundreds of GYPO Pretties to share their all-time favorite winter outfit formulas. Check out their top three choices and what they had to say.

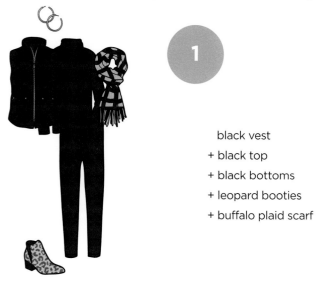

1

black vest
+ black top
+ black bottoms
+ leopard booties
+ buffalo plaid scarf

"This became my go-to outfit this winter! I was easily able to dress up and dress down the same basic formula." —Cindy G. (age 53)

"This outfit formula screams sophistication with the black column of color and the pops of pattern with the plaid scarf and the leopard booties." —Lisa B. (age 56)

"I didn't expect to like this formula when I first got the capsule, but I loved the way it looked on me. The monochromatic look was so sophisticated. The buffalo plaid was a natural pair, but the leopard was unexpected and fun! The first time I wore this outfit, a friend asked me what big plans I had because she thought I was dressed up." —Jessica K. (age 39)

2

black jacket
+ graphic sweatshirt
+ black bottoms
+ white sneakers
+ buffalo plaid scarf

"Comfy and cozy vibe; ready for staying in or heading outside for a little winter fun!" —Maraline F. (age 60)

"Casual enough for working at home but easy to dress up for a night out." —Tara H. (age 45)

"It's warm and cozy but still has fun and details." —Sarah G. (age 38)

3

black vest
+ plaid top
+ gray top
+ black bottoms
+ black booties

"This was such an easy outfit to put together with items from my closet that I would not have thought to put together before. This outfit made me feel so...put together!" —Charlene C. (age 49)

"Black pants with a vest and a plaid or striped shirt—so classic. I wear this type of thing all the time. It feels timeless to me." —Lynn B. (age 58)

"We don't have much winter here in the desert, so a vest is just enough warmth yet still on trend." —Kellye W. (age 53)

wool coat
+ sweater dress
+ black tights
+ black boots

wool coat
+ neutral sweater
+ chambray shirt
+ gray jeans
+ riding boots

solid sweater
+ printed scarf
+ black jeans
+ black boots

neutral cardigan
+ striped top
+ gray jeans
+ leopard boots

163

puffer jacket
+ black turtleneck
+ gray jeans
+ rugged boots

puffer jacket
+ neutral sweater
+ plaid scarf
+ black jeans
+ rugged boots

A few years back I introduced the infamously polarizing fur vest. Some thought it made them feel like a yeti; others loved it to pieces. I fell into the latter category. This outfit ended up being one of my favorites that winter. Fur vest not your thing? No problem! Simply skip this top layer or sub a faux fur scarf.

'Tis the season to shine! Wear your sparkle with an everyday look by pairing it with casual basics, like a cardigan, jeans, and flats.

fur vest + neutral sweater + burgundy jeans + riding boots

Winter pastels are fresh and modern. Try this pairing with a blush pink sweater and a cozy gray long cardigan.

neutral cardigan + solid sweater + dark-wash jeans + riding boots

No two ways about it—faux leather leggings make me feel fierce! Yes, I understand they're not for everyone, but pairing them up with a long tunic sweater definitely increases the comfort level. Try this sweater in cobalt blue or any jewel tone. Leopard booties will pair perfectly with it!

wool coat + tunic sweater + leggings + leopard booties

It's the most wonderful time of the year. No matter how you plan to make merry, these special-occasion outfits will be sure to fashionably fit the bill.

black cardigan + solid blouse + plaid pants + black heels

Winter is the perfect time to play with fabric textures in your outfit. Mix up knits, velvet, and silk to add interest and depth to your look.

fur coat + plaid sheath dress + black heels

wool coat + black blouse + black velvet pants + leopard booties

This one stands on its own even without the fur vest, although in my opinion, you don't want to skip it. It's an outfit maker for sure!

fur vest
+ black blouse
+ burgundy jeans
+ ankle boots

Here's a date-night outfit formula that always works: Pair any jewel-toned blouse with black skinny jeans and ankle boots, and add a statement necklace. Voilà!

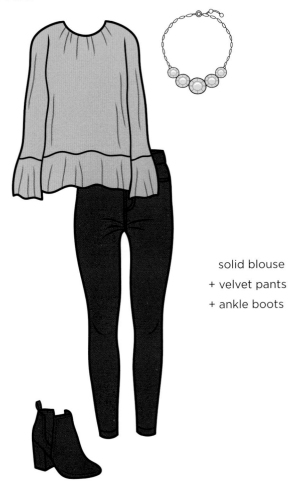

solid blouse
+ velvet pants
+ ankle boots

Are you seeing a pattern here? Black and burgundy is a hot combo for winter date nights. Nothing complements it quite like leopard print.

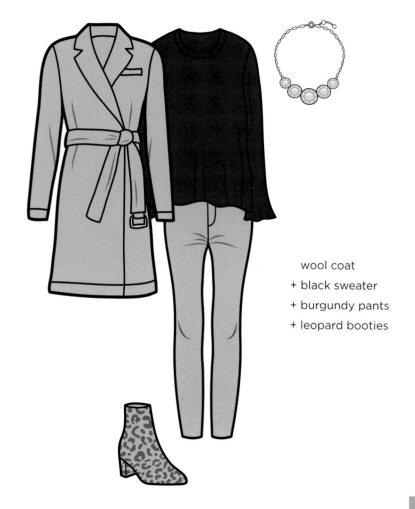

wool coat
+ black sweater
+ burgundy pants
+ leopard booties

Bonus—Holiday Party Dressing Tips

1. All black is always a good idea. It's foolproof and can be easily dressed up or down. Plus it's always chic and in style. Or take it one step further and add a wrap or cape in a bold print, like leopard or red buffalo check.

2. Add one piece of bling to any outfit. Choose one piece of jewelry to be your showstopper, and keep everything else subtle so it doesn't compete. Wear a bold statement necklace with delicate stud earrings or flashy chandelier earrings with a simple bracelet stack.

3. If ever there was an occasion to go bold with your lipstick, the holidays are it! Your local beauty store can help you find the perfect red for your complexion, and you'll be ready to dance the night away.

Legging Looks You'll Love

Before we move on from winter outfit formulas, let me preface this by saying yes, *GYPO* started as a way to help me get out of my yoga-pants rut. But leggings are an entirely different thing, especially when paired up with the right formula. They are perfect for lounging on the couch or going out to brunch with friends. They are also a quintessential item for the fall and winter months because they are cozy, they are comfortable, and they are stretchy and perfectly forgiving, which is ideal for all those fantastic holiday meals and treats.

My go-to for leggings are my faux leather leggings. They are the easiest, most comfortable way to amp up any of my leggings outfits. They are truly a game-changer. Below I'm sharing five different looks that utilize either black or faux leather leggings to keep you stylish and comfortable all winter long. I love leggings so much I created a guide full of outfit formulas that feature them! The looks here are a sampling of those outfits, and you can head to getyourprettyon.com/book to get the rest of the looks for free!

  neutral cardigan
+ graphic tee
+ white sneakers

chambray button-down
+ white tee
+ leopard ankle boots

striped turtleneck
+ black vest
+ rugged boots
+ pom-pom beanie

denim jacket
+ camo or printed tee
+ black ankle boots

raincoat
+ striped top
+ rain boots

9

DRESS IT UP

Not gonna lie—in addition to my amazing coworkers, one of the few things I miss about my stint in corporate America is getting dressed up. Oh how I adored my wardrobe of pencil skirts, feminine blouses, and those heels. *So. Many. Pairs.* To be honest, I miss the look of them, but my feet don't miss spending all day crammed into them!

Although my professional attire takes up far less space in my closet these days, I do still need a few go-to items in there for the variety of events, conferences, and other occasions that require me to step outside of my work-from-home-mom life.

DRESS-IT-UP CLOSET STAPLE ESSENTIALS

So what does a girl need in her closet when it's time to gussy up a bit? Here's a list of my dress-it-up closet staple essentials:

ALISON'S AWESOME ADVICE
Mixed metals are super stylish.
Try mixing silver and gold or rose gold.

STRIPED SHIRT

WHITE BUTTON-DOWN SHIRT

BLACK TOP

BLACK-AND-WHITE
PRINTED BLOUSE

TOP SOLID BLOUSE

SOLID SWEATER

BRIGHT CARDIGAN

MOTO JACKET

PRINTED PANTS

WHITE PANTS

BLACK PANTS

BRIGHT PANTS

DARK-WASH JEANS

NAVY SKIRT

BLACK-AND-WHITE
PRINTED SKIRT

SOLID DRESS

BLACK BLAZER

MYTH:

Moto jackets are only for casual outfits and have no place in the office.

TRUTH:

A moto jacket is an awesome substitution for your basic blazer and can be a great way to update your look. Try layering one over a sheath dress to give it a little edge.

MYTH:

Bold prints and patterns are not acceptable in a professional environment.

TRUTH:

Prints and patterns are fair game anytime, as long as they are done tastefully. If you are concerned about a print being 'too much' follow these guidelines. Choose one print and keep the rest of your look neutral – think a printed blouse paired with a solid skirt and nude heels. Keep your prints and patterns to traditional classics like polka dots, florals, leopard, or stripes. Test the waters with something small like printed shoes, a neck scarf, or a handbag.

MYTH:

Wearing heels all day is too uncomfortable.

TRUTH:

Try wearing a wider block heel or wedge style for all day comfort.

DRESS-IT-UP SHOPPING LIST

With the items on this shopping list, you'll be able to create any of the dressy outfit formulas that follow. Don't forget to shop your closet first, and always choose shoes that are functional for your lifestyle.

TOPS

Printed	☐
Black	☐
White	☐
Floral	☐
Blue Oxford Shirt	☐
Striped Button Down	☐
Neutral Sweater	☐

BOTTOMS

Can be jeans, skirts, or pants.

Black	☐
Patterned	☐
Solid Color	☐
Gray	☐
Plaid	☐

LAYERS

Bright Cardigan	☐
Trench Coat	☐
Moto Jacket	☐
Black Blazer	☐
Gray Blazer	☐

DRESSES

| Solid Dress | ☐ |

FOOTWEAR

Choose the type of footwear that works best for your lifestyle.

Leopard	☐
Bright	☐
Neutral	☐
Printed	☐

ACCESSORIES

Hoop Earrings	☐
Pendant Necklace	☐
Statement Necklace	☐
Statement Earrings	☐
Short Delicate Necklace	☐
Stud Earrings	☐

For a printable version of this shopping list that you can check off, visit getyourprettyon.com/book.

bright cardigan + printed blouse + black pants + leopard shoes

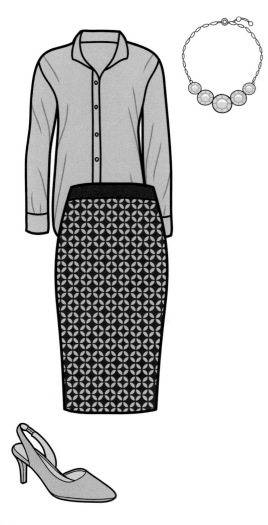

blue oxford + printed skirt + bright shoes

trench coat + striped button-down + black skirt + leopard shoes

moto jacket + printed top + black pants + bright shoes

black top + colored pants + neutral shoes

solid dress + neutral heels

moto jacket + white blouse + black pants + neutral heels

bright cardigan + black top + printed skirt + leopard shoes

black blazer + printed top + bright pants + leopard shoes

gray blazer + striped button-down + bright skirt + leopard shoes

neutral sweater + printed pants + bright shoes

gray blazer + black top + gray skirt + printed or neutral shoes

LITTLE BLACK DRESS

Let's talk about the little black dress (LBD). The LBD is a tried-and-true closet staple that everyone really should have in their wardrobe arsenal. Don't let the term "little" confuse you. When I say "little," I don't mean something skimpy that you wore in your twenties or something that you wear only once every five years. The term LBD simply means a versatile black dress that you could easily pull out for church, a wedding, a fancy date night, or an event. It's there for the happy events that take us by surprise, but it can also provide us a quick outfit solution for more somber occasions as well.

Your LBD should make you feel comfortable and can be as simple as a sheath dress or something with a little more detail. I bought my favorite LBD on Amazon for $39, so it really doesn't have to be expensive either. Just pick a classic silhouette and accessorize it, and just like magic, it will become perfect for any event. Check out some of my favorite LBD outfit formulas!

moto jacket
+ black dress
+ black ankle boots

"One is never overdressed or underdressed with a little black dress."

—KARL LAGERFELD

faux fur jacket
+ black dress
+ bright color heels

black cardigan
+ black dress
+ leopard heels

10

ACCESSORIES AND FOOTWEAR

Accessories are the spice of your outfits. They add that dash of something extra that takes your outfit formula to the next level. I love the way every woman can express her individuality by adding the perfect accessories to her look.

Maybe you're a minimalist like me. If so, just a delicate necklace and pair of hoop or stud earrings could be all you need on a daily basis. I tend not to pile on accessories unless it's a special occasion.

But maybe you love a good stack of arm-candy bracelets, or big earrings are your signature look, or you can't leave the house without a ring on every finger. There's no right or wrong when it comes to your accessory style. If you follow a few simple rules, you can be perfectly accessorized every time.

> **ALISON'S AWESOME ADVICE**
> Matchy-matchy is outdated. Your purse and
> shoes no longer need to match!.

TIPS FOR PAIRING JEWELRY

When it comes to necklaces and earrings, remember these three formulas for foolproof pairing:

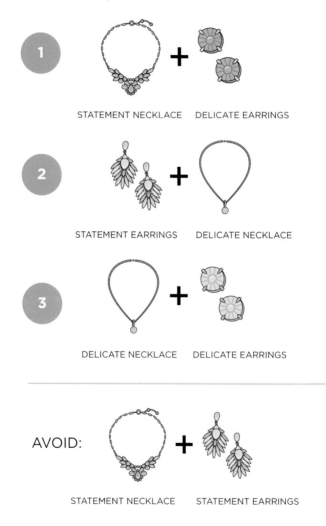

1 STATEMENT NECKLACE + DELICATE EARRINGS

2 STATEMENT EARRINGS + DELICATE NECKLACE

3 DELICATE NECKLACE + DELICATE EARRINGS

AVOID: STATEMENT NECKLACE + STATEMENT EARRINGS

Here's a list of some closet staple essential accessories:

HOOP EARRINGS

STUD EARRINGS

DELICATE SHORT
NECKLACE

LONG PENDANT
NECKLACE

STATEMENT
NECKLACE

STATEMENT EARRINGS

BANGLE BRACELET

WRAP BRACELET

Your accessories should complement your clothing, not compete with it. Not sure which necklace to style with your top? This reference chart will guide you to the perfect bling for the occasion!

NECKLACE/NECKLINE GUIDE

BOAT NECK
LONG BEADS

COLLARED SHIRT
PENDANT OR CHOKER

COWL
STATEMENT EARRINGS

CREW NECK
BIB OR COLLAR

HALTER NECK
SLIM PENDANTS

OFF-SHOULDER
ASYMMETRIC

SCOOP
SHORTER PENDANTS
WITH VOLUME

SQUARE CUT
ANGULAR PENDANTS

STRAPLESS
CHOKER

SWEETHEART
CARVED BEADS
OR PENDANTS

TURTLENECK
LONG CHAINS
OR PENDANTS

V-NECK
V-SHAPED PENDANT

OTHER ACCESSORY TYPES

Scarves

Scarves seem to come in and out of vogue and have a moment every few years. They are considered a closet staple in my book. If you have an extensive collection of classic scarves, hold on to it. Even if they aren't the most popular girl in high school right now, give them a few years, and they'll come back around.

There are many different scarf types and varieties out there—from immense blanket scarves to chic neck scarves and infinity scarves. One of the biggest questions I get is how the heck to tie the thing. Lucky for us, there are a plethora of YouTubers just waiting for you to jump online and watch their clever tutorials, which are *way* more helpful than anything I could try to describe here. So go ahead, take a few minutes, and look up some scarf-tying tutorials. I promise to be here when you come back.

If wearing a scarf around your neck just isn't for you, there are other options for styling this accessory. Tie a small scarf around the handle of your purse, around your wrist in lieu of a bracelet, or around the elastic of your ponytail as a playful finishing touch to your look.

Scarves not your thing? Feel like they're too suffocating? Don't want to wear them indoors? That's OK. You can still add interest to your outfit and look put together by substituting a statement necklace for a scarf.

Bags

When it comes to your daily handbag, there's just one rule: It must be functional for *your* lifestyle.

That's really all that matters. Who cares about the latest "it" bag if "it" doesn't work for you? I'm all for trying the latest trends, but if they leave you feeling uncomfortable or frustrated, it's totally fine to decide they're not for you. This applies not only to bags but to all beauty and fashion trends. The important thing is that you tried something outside your comfort zone, and that alone is worth celebrating!

I recommend every woman has the following bags in her collection:

1. **A daily workhorse.** This can be an all-purpose tote, hobo, or any other style of bag that carries your daily essentials. Be sure it is well organized inside, has a pocket for your cell phone, and makes it easy to grab anything else you need at your fingertips. Tip: If your purse is cavernous, you can find a handy-dandy organizer insert on Amazon for a steal! Bonus: If you want to switch up your purses, all you have to do is move your organizer from the old one to the new one. Presto chango!

2. **A dress-up bag.** This can be a clutch or smaller, dressier purse of any type. Make sure there's enough room for your phone, compact, and lip gloss.

Not a fan of switching out your purse? You don't have to. Invest in a well-made neutral leather bag that you can carry year-round.

Footwear

There's no doubt about it—great shoes take you great places. Having the right shoes in your closet is more about what works for your lifestyle than what the trends dictate you should be wearing. Most of us are not going to chase toddlers in three-inch stiletto heels. Likewise, frumpy flats won't flatter a killer dress.

When I left corporate America, one of the hardest wardrobe rebuilding efforts was in the area of footwear. At one point I had nearly 60 pairs of heels in my closet and almost no flats! Suddenly my life changed dramatically, and my sneakers became my go-to everyday shoes. As with my yoga pants, it wasn't because I was doing anything athletic; it was more a matter of what was readily available. Sadly, my sneakers were the only comfortable flat shoes in my closet.

I slowly started to build my footwear wardrobe for my work-from-home lifestyle. The first pair of shoes I invested in was a good quality pair of leopard-print flats. Over the years, I've replaced those flats multiple times and added leopard-print wedges, sandals, and even ankle boots. (Remember, leopard is a neutral!)

I've gradually acquired a functional and fashionable footwear collection that works perfectly for my daily life, special events, and everything in between.

When it comes to building your footwear collection, keep these two rules in mind:

1. Invest in quality-made shoes that are also comfortable. On a cost-per-wear basis, it pays to spend a little more for quality footwear.
2. Buy multiple styles in colors and patterns that will work with most everything. Just like I did with my leopard-print shoes, you may want to also add in several different styles of metallic, black, neutral, and brightly colored shoes. Wedges, heels, flats, sandals, sneakers, and ankle boots are the styles that I wear most often.

Here's a list of closet staple essentials footwear:

WEDGES

KITTEN HEELS

STILETTOS

BLOCK HEELS

BALLET FLATS

MULES

LOAFERS

FLAT SANDALS

HEELED SANDALS

ANKLE BOOTS

RIDING BOOTS

RUGGED BOOTS

(if you live somewhere
with a true winter)

ATHLETIC SHOES

WHITE SNEAKERS

SLIP-ON SNEAKERS

Once you have your footwear basics in place, I recommend getting metallic, leopard, black, neutral, bright, and printed shoes in various styles to add even more styling options to your wardrobe.

Bonus—How to Wear Ankle Boots

One FAQ of *GYPO* readers through the years has been about how to wear ankle boots. I get it; they're tricky. Do you cuff your jeans above them? Do they work with jeans that aren't skinny? Can you pair them with dresses and skirts?

Here are some ideas that will help you become an ankle boot expert:

1. **The socks.** Wear a pair of low-cut socks, like ankle socks or no-show socks.

2. **With skinny jeans**. If your jeans are the right length and hit just above the ankle boot, you shouldn't need to cuff them. Remember, ankle boots pair well with ankle jeans. (Funny how that works, right?) It's also OK if they scrunch up a bit at the bottom. You can always tuck them into the top of the boots. The best look, though, is with just a bit of skin showing at the ankle. Of course, cuffing your jeans is an option if they're too long. Just be sure the cuff hits just above the ankle boot without too much skin showing.

3. **With other jeans and pants.** You can also pair up your ankle boots with flared, straight leg, and wider leg styles of pants. Wear the ankle boot under the pant leg and be sure your pants nearly skim the floor for the best look.

4. **With skirts and dresses.** Ankle boots pair seamlessly with most skirts and dresses. No rules to follow here—just slip them on and you're good to go!

11

MASTER-CLASS-LEVEL STYLE

Most women in my Outfit Formulas styling program start out following each outfit formula to the letter, interpreting it as literally as possible. As time goes on, they start to experiment with variables, like subbing for colors they love or accessorizing differently or adding in touches of their own personal style. Eventually they reach a master-level of style confidence, and that, my friend, is a beautiful sight to see! It's honestly one of the most rewarding parts of this whole process for me. Nothing is more fulfilling than watching a woman learn to confidently style herself and begin to feel empowered in her fashion choices.

Nothing is more fulfilling than watching a woman learn to confidently style herself and begin to feel empowered in her fashion choices.

You may not be there yet, and that's totally understandable. But one day you may feel like you want a little something more, so I've put together some master-level style tips and tricks in this chapter for you to experiment with.

STYLE MAKERS—IT'S THE LITTLE THINGS!

In chapter 2 we covered the steps to defining your personal style. Now we're going to talk about some style makers, which are the hallmarks of each style type. These are useful when you're ready to make an outfit formula feel like your own. By adding or substituting elements from your personal style type below, you can tweak the outfit formula to put your own true-to-you spin on it.

Classic. Most of the outfit formulas in this book are classic. There's a reason for that—longevity. Classic looks tend to stay in style! What good is a book on style if it's irrelevant after one or two seasons? If you lean toward classic style, you can interpret these outfits pretty literally and most likely be happy as a clam. However, if you want to take it to the next level, you could experiment with one or more of the categories of classic style—like preppy, vintage, ladylike, or French style.

Preppy. Building blocks of preppy style include girly blouses, blazers, Mary Jane heels, pearls, sheath dresses, printed cardigans, statement necklaces, A-line and pencil skirts, ballet flats, colored chinos, and skinny belts.

Vintage. Choose your favorite decade and add style elements from it, like vintage-style dresses, brooches, handbags, blouses, A-line skirts, cocktail dresses, hats, pumps, and skirt suits.

Ladylike. Items with ruffles, lace, or bows; heels of all types; full, pleated, or pencil skirts; frilly blouses; floral prints; ballet flats; red lips; boxy jackets; and pink anything.

French. Ooh la la! Add a dash of French classic style with a little black dress, oxford shirts, silk shirts, straight-leg pants and jeans, a beige trench coat, blazers, silk blouses, striped tops, oversized sweaters, wrap dresses, tailored pants, or silk scarves.

Bohemian. Sprinkle in some tassels, fringe, and paisley prints. Look for natural, earthy materials in your jewelry. Other elements include maxi skirts, suede ankle boots, headwraps and headbands, printed maxi dresses, gladiator sandals, knit cardigans and sweaters, floppy hats, tunic tees and blouses, geometric prints, and hobo bags.

Minimal. Less is more when it comes to minimalist style. Stick to your basics with a classic wool coat, quality knits in cashmere, button-down shirts, great-fitting jeans, form-fitting tees, an LBD, well-tailored blazers, nude and black heels, diamond stud earrings, or black ankle boots.

Eclectic. Think outside the box to mix and match pieces you already own, like graphic tees with a leopard-print skirt, or tough-girl moto jackets with ladylike lace skirts and shirts. Mix patterns and prints—like floral with pol-ka dots or stripes with animal prints. Combine sneakers with a skirt or dress, T-shirts with frilly skirts, or chunky knit sweaters over dresses. Mix metals in jewelry...and *have fun*!

PATTERN MIXING

Pattern mixing done well is a fine art to be sure. It's another one of those comfort-zone busters that intimidates Outfit Formulas members at first and then, nine times out of ten, becomes fan favorite. Nailing down that sweet spot of color, scale, and print is tricky, but if you follow a few simple guidelines, your odds of discovering the perfect combination are high. Just as master chefs constantly taste as they cook, try on your outfit as you explore mixing patterns. Sometimes it's hard to get the right per-ception just looking at your clothing, but wearing it will give you the full experience. This is another time when taking a selfie is incredibly helpful too. Mix patterns like a pro with these three pattern-mixing tips!

1. Match at least one color. When mixing patterns, try to keep at least one coordinating color between the two patterns. This helps give some continuity to your outfit even though the patterns are different.

NAVY & WHITE
STRIPED TOP

RED FLORAL
TOP WITH
WHITE & BLACK

NAVY, WHITE,
BLACK & BLUE
FLORAL BOTTOM

BLACK & WHITE
PLAID BOTTOM

2. **Vary your pattern print size.** Mix up your pattern sizes. Do either a large-print bottom and small-print top or vice versa. If your prints are too similar in scale, the eye won't know where to look first.

WIDE STRIPE TOP

SMALL POLKA
DOT PRINT

SMALL POLKA
DOT BOTTOMS

LARGE
FLORAL PRINT

3. Follow the formula. Every pattern falls into a category of being either busy and complex or clean and simple. When in doubt, follow one of these two formulas when mixing your patterns, and you can't go wrong!

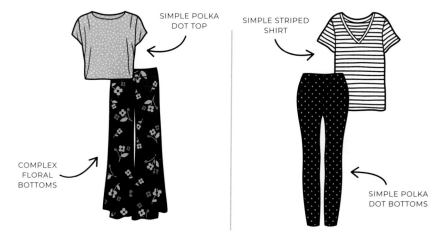

SIMPLE POLKA
DOT TOP

SIMPLE STRIPED
SHIRT

COMPLEX
FLORAL
BOTTOMS

SIMPLE POLKA
DOT BOTTOMS

simple + complex

simple + simple

In the world of pattern mixing, think of stripes as a neutral. With their clean lines and simple pattern, they can be mixed with just about anything!

FINISHING TOUCHES

We all know women who look incredibly put together and stylish. But have you ever noticed that when you attempt to replicate their look, it somehow just falls flat? Womp womp. But I'm willing to bet that the only things separating your look and hers are the finishing touches.

These small details are what give an outfit the polished, pulled together, and intentionally styled look that you see on fashion blogs, retailer websites, and maybe even that super-stylish friend you would love to emulate. Think of it like an ice cream sundae without the cherry on top...who wants that! (Unless you despise cherries, that is. I'm a whipped-cream girl myself.)

Here are a few finishing touches to consider adding to your ensemble before you walk out the door:

- **Roll the cuffs of your long shirt sleeves,** especially if you are wearing a layering piece underneath. Having the base layer peek out at your cuff is a cute accent detail. Search Pinterest for the "J.Crew cuff fold" tutorial—this technique is a classic mannequin styling trick of retail merchandisers everywhere.

- **Pop a collar,** especially if you are wearing a layering piece over your collar. Nothing highlights a crisp, polished blouse quite like it. And while we are talking about collars, consider wearing your statement necklace tucked under your collar. Button your shirt all the way up except the top button, flip up your collar, add your statement necklace, and then fold your collar back down. It may feel a little strange at first, but you just never know whether it's for you until you try it.

- **Mix up textures and silhouettes.** If a basic tee or top is feeling too bland, look for one that offers an extra notion of interest. Think ruffles, lace, or eyelets for simple feminine touches. Or if you are feeling a little bit daring, try a bolder silhouette, like bell sleeves or puff shoulders.

- **There's nothing quite like a touch of something unexpected.** A burst of color, pattern, or texture can elevate your look and really showcase your stylish creativity. A dash of animal print in your leopard flats, sneakers with a colorful stripe detail, or a purse with a funky tassel are all great ways to keep your look engaging.

- **Create dynamic interest by breaking up solid blocks of color.** Consider adding a front tuck or a knot to the hem of your top to break up that solid horizontal line across your middle. You can add a knot in the center of your body, or you can pull the knot to the side if you prefer a bit of extra tummy coverage.

- **Show your pants some cuff love too!** Rolling and cuffing isn't just for your tops; your jeans can take advantage of this styling tip as well. Your technique here will vary depending on your footwear, but experiment with different looks, like a wide cuff, a narrow, rolled cuff, or even a pegged cuff à la the '80s. Funny how every trend comes back around, isn't it?

A word of caution—don't try to incorporate all these tips into one look. Part of perfecting a look is knowing when to call it done. It's an art for certain, but as they say, practice makes perfect! And as I always say, when in doubt, take a selfie. The selfie never lies!

GET THE RIGHT FIT

I touched on discovering and celebrating your body shape in chapter 3, so if you skimmed over that section earlier, now is the time to go back and bust out your measuring tape. Learning how to best flatter your figure is one of the quickest ways to elevate your style and your confidence. Choosing silhouettes that enhance your shape in all the right places is the quickest way to look amazing, feel incredible, and slim your body. You can save time and money by knowing exactly what style of pieces to look for and what gets a hard pass, and you'll fall even more in love with the wardrobe you have curated. Who doesn't want that!

Foundation garments that fit you correctly are critical to everything sitting just where it should and enhancing your curves in just the right way. If it's been a while since your last bra fitting, inquire at your local department store or lingerie boutique for a proper fitting. They are typically offered free of charge and don't take more than a few minutes. This is an easy update that will make a huge difference in the final look of your outfit of the day.

CONCLUSION

Remember that secret I shared with you way back in the introduction? Well, we're pretty much besties by now, so here's another one.

I don't have a burning passion for style, and I don't even like to shop. *What!*

It's not uncommon for me to wear the same outfit three times in one week. That's why you rarely see pics of me on social media wearing my latest and greatest buys.

Yet I make a living as a style blogger, I wrote this book about style, and I've built a first-of-its-kind online styling program with nearly 50,000 members (and counting).

Why would anyone come to me for style advice?

Since I hate to shop and put together outfits, I created a program to make it easy—not just for me but for you too. I want you to walk into a store armed with a shopping list so you don't wander aimlessly. Because that's what I want. I want everything you buy to be paired up in multiple ways, getting you the most bang for your buck. Because that's what I want. I want you to open your closet knowing that you have go-to outfit formulas that make your life easier. Because that's what I want. I want you to feel confident in *everything* you wear. Because that's what I want. I want your clothes and shoes to suit *your* lifestyle, not what some fashion guru or magazine tells you to wear. Because that's what I want.

Want to know another secret? The simplest outfits are the ones I wear the most. At the heart of it all, I'm truly a T-shirt and jeans kind of girl. It works for my life, and it makes me feel awesome.

I don't have a passion for style, but I do have a passion for making life easier—yours and mine. But most important, I'm passionate about you feeling confident in your clothes, just as you are, right now. Style is for all of us—no exceptions.

If you walk away with just one thing from this book, I want it to be this—confidence and a sense that you deserve to do what it takes to live your most beautiful life. *You are worthy*. You are wonderfully made by your Creator. Never, ever forget this.

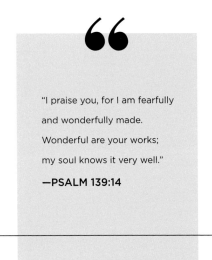

"I praise you, for I am fearfully and wonderfully made. Wonderful are your works; my soul knows it very well."

—PSALM 139:14

NOTES

Introduction

1 Matthew Hutson and Tori Rodriguez, "Dress for Success: How Clothes Influence Our Performance," *Scientific American*, January 1, 2016, https://www.scientificamerican.com/article/dress-for-success-how -clothes-influence-our-performance/.

2 Hajo Adam and Adam D. Galinsky, "Enclothed Cognition," *Journal of Experimental Social Psychology* 48, no. 4 (2012): 918–925, https://doi .org/10.1016/j.jesp.2012.02.008.

3 Joel Hoomans, "35,000 Decisions: The Great Choices of Strategic Leaders," The Leading Edge, https://go.roberts.edu/leadingedge/ the-great-choices-of-strategic-leaders.

4 "Capsule wardrobe," Wikipedia, https://en.wikipedia.org/wiki/ Capsule_wardrobe.

Chapter 2: Making it Your Own—Define Your Personal Style

5 Megan LaRussa, "The Four Main Personal Style Types," Style Yourself Chic with Megan LaRussa, https://www.styleyourselfchic.com/ types-of-clothing-styles/.

Chapter 3: Dressing Your Body Shape

6 Bradley Bayou, *The Science of Sexy: Dress to Fit Your Unique Figure with the Style System That Works for Every Shape and Size* (New York, NY: Gotham Books, 2007).

MY OUTFIT NOTES

MY OUTFIT NOTES

LIFE-CHANGING CONFIDENCE
FROM THE GYPO COMMUNITY

"It is difficult for me to put into words how very much GYPO and the style challenges have impacted my life. I had little sense of style and depended on my daughter to help me look somewhat stylish and put together. Thanks to Alison Lumbatis, her great style expertise, and the challenges, I now can put together an outfit quickly and feel totally put together. What a confidence booster it has been!" —Carol Bibb Jamison

"GYPO has made such a difference for me! I used to have more clothes than I knew what to do with and nothing to wear. GYPO takes the work out of getting dressed. I know what works together, and I get lots of compliments on my outfits. My mornings are simplified thanks to GYPO!" —Amy Bishop

"This has been so helpful to me! As a busy homeschool mom of four, I don't have a lot of time to think about fashion. I do appreciate feeling put together, though! With Get Your Pretty On, all of the hard work has already been done for me, so I can focus on other things!" —Amanda Bare

"Participating in the GYPO challenges has been one of the best things I have done! They have helped me create a closet of clothes I love, have more confidence in myself, pick and choose colors that work for me instead of against me, and find a wonderful community of Pretties who are so special." —Maraline McLaughlin Freeman

"Love this! You can modify the outfits for your daily needs so easily. I keep these calendars in my closet for reference. Fabulous—classic but trendy!" —Lisa Caroline Rose Scott

"This is my second GYPO challenge, and I can say I'm 100 percent hooked! Between the shopping list with a variety of different options geared to fit any budget, lifestyle, and body size; the daily outfits, which make getting dressed every day fun; and the supportive Facebook groups, what's not to love? These challenges have given me the confidence to try new pieces I would have never picked out before and wear them like a pro. I've gotten tons of compliments on my new fashion choices, and my kids and husband love my new looks. The boost these challenges have given my confidence has been well worth it. If you are on the fence about giving one of these challenges a try, take the jump and do it! I promise you won't regret it!" —Jennifer Conway

ABOUT ALISON

Alison Lumbatis is the founder and CEO of Get Your Pretty On® and Outfit Formulas®, a first-of-its-kind personal styling framework. She's served more than 50,000 women through the Outfit Formulas® program and has attracted an online audience of millions to the *GYPO* blog. Her platform democratizes style for every body and budget and is a leading resource to help women rediscover their worthiness through wardrobe.

An author and certified life coach, Alison is a thought leader in the personal style and confidence arenas. She's been featured in *Forbes*, *Redbook*, and *Life & Style* magazines. A sought-after speaker and podcast guest, Alison speaks on fighting feelings of unworthiness and the power of "prioritizing pretty." She lives in Flower Mound, Texas, with her husband, Craig, their three children, Devon, Aubrey, and Ava, and three dogs, three cats, two donkeys, and a horse.

Connect with Alison online at alisonlumbatis.com.